Waking Up In
NEW YORK CITY

Printed and bound in Great Britain by MPG Books Ltd,
Bodmin, Cornwall

Distributed in the US by Publishers Group West

Published by Sanctuary Publishing Limited, Sanctuary House,
45–53 Sinclair Road, London W14 0NS, United Kingdom

www.sanctuarypublishing.com

ISBN: 1-86074-531-8

Waking Up In
NEW YORK CITY

Mike Evans

Sanctuary

Contents

Acknowledgements

In addition to the books, periodicals and websites acknowledged as source material in the Bibliography, a big thank you to Todd Abramson at Telstar Records, Paul Colby at the Bitter End, Ted Gottfried at See Hear, Percy Jones and Joyce Francis, Hilly Kristal at CBGB, Lach at Fortified Records, Gary Olson, Allan Pepper at the Bottom Line, Rob Sacher at LunaSea Records, John Schroeder and Jack Earl at Rudy's Bar & Grill, Brian Turner at WFMU, Shay Visha at the Knitting Factory, and Iain MacGregor and Chris Harvey at Sanctuary Publishing. Not forgetting Anna for being a patient editor, and Lizzie for unravelling the tapes.

Mike Evans, August 2003

Introduction

The earliest memory I have of anything to do with New York City was a picture of the Empire State Building. It was a jigsaw-like cut-out made of gummed paper, which I caringly pieced together bit by bit, until, window after window, floor after floor, it was complete. Towering into a perfect blue sky, it fascinated me even then. It was indefinably perfect, and in the context of 1940s Britain, definitively modern. I must have been six or seven years old.

I didn't know then it was New York, but it was certainly the Empire State even though the name of the building didn't register at the time, at least not that I remember. But the picture was indelible. Among the thousands of images that install themselves in the memory at that formative age, most sink into the unconscious – some to be retrieved when needed – otherwise our minds would be too cluttered to take in anything more. Others, for one reason or another, stay with us for the rest of our lives.

The next recollection I have of Manhattan, which must have been around the same time, also centred on the Empire State Building, when my father took me to a local cinema to see the already antiquated early-'30s blockbuster *King Kong*. The sequences of the gargantuan ape rampaging through New York and scaling the tallest building in the world were among the earliest in a childhood full of images absorbed in the dark of the 'picture house' – images, it has to be said, that were predominantly American.

From there on in, New York simply came to represent the ultimate big city, its architecture iconographic of the 20th century – not just the

Empire State, but the Chrysler Building, the Woolworth Building, the Rockefeller Center and so on. And among the most enduring images of these first years of the 21st century must be the fire-engulfed twin towers of the World Trade Center on that fateful day in September '01.

New York has been fictionalised as Superman's Metropolis and Batman's Gotham City, stylised in a thousand movies from Elia Kazan's *On The Waterfront* to Martin Scorsese's *Taxi Driver*, and romanticised in song and dance through *Guys And Dolls* and *West Side Story* to *42nd Street* and *New York, New York*.

It's been celebrated in music as diverse as George Gershwin's 'Rhapsody In Blue', Rodgers and Hart's 'Manhattan', Leiber and Stoller's 'On Broadway' and Ellington's 'Take The A Train', not to mention 'Spanish Harlem Incident' from Bob Dylan, The Strokes' 'New York City Cops', and The Ad Libs' 'The Boy From New York City'. And of course not forgetting The Velvet Underground's 'Waiting For The Man', plus 'Coney Island Baby' and 'NYC Man' by Lou Reed.

To paraphrase The Beatles' 'Penny Lane', New York has been very much in my ears and in my eyes for almost as long as I can remember, its landscape and even its atmosphere weirdly familiar long before I ever set foot on its streets.

For the visitor, the initial sight of New York – or more specifically Manhattan – can take the breath away. And that's not just on the first-time visit. Every time the skyline swings into vision on the cab ride across Queens from JFK Airport, or even more spectacularly along the opposite banks of the Hudson if you're coming in from Newark, New Jersey, the buzz is there. Likewise emerging from the Midtown Tunnel into the canyon of 42nd Street is like entering no other city on earth. And waking up in New York can be even better.

The exhilaration of just 'hitting the streets' on a crisp cold morning in winter, or getting to Central Park before the crowds when the heat is still comfortable in springtime, are simple pleasures rivalled only by the ritual of a New York breakfast of ham, eggs and coffee. And after the briefest of stays in Manhattan you can't fail to be aware of how much of the character of the City, the social fabric, is coloured by the attitudes of New Yorkers themselves.

Despite layers of sophistication, a rich cultural history and some serious – and very conspicuous – wealth, New York is basically a working-class city, most residents living in the outer boroughs, going about their daily lives, famous for their straight-talking directness (not to be confused with rudeness), sense of humour and a 'no-nonsense' attitude. The UK parallels would be with the provincial working-class cities of Liverpool or Newcastle – both of which have a tradition of a staunch independence of spirit – rather than the capital, but the similarity ends there.

So the idea of writing a book based on the notion of waking up in New York, hitting the streets and talking to people, had an instant appeal. The additional factor, the brief being for the book to have a musical dimension, was the other reason the publishers approached me in the first place.

Since the birth of Tin Pan Alley – identified historically with the Brill Building on Broadway – and the days when jazz clubs dominated uptown Harlem and midtown 52nd Street, New York City has been at the cutting edge of musical activity. Added to that, a cultural and ethnic mix more diverse than in any other place on earth has resulted in a similar musical 'melting pot' in the City.

Although the centres of the US music industry business-wise have always been geographically spread between an East and West Coast concentration in New York and Los Angeles, with other places like Nashville and Detroit representing specific sections of the industry, New York is particularly rich in actual musical activity, from recording studios to clubs to major concert venues, and remains so today.

This applies not just to commercial rock music but across the board in areas as diverse as hip-hop, jazz, avant-garde and folk music, plus ethnically based genres from Cuba, Puerto Rico and other Latin American scenes to the 'Klezmer' styles with its roots in East European Jewish music.

An early passion for jazz, swiftly taking over from movies as a preoccupation of my teenage years, made New York an even more evocative symbol than it had been via the cinema. Although it was given that the music had its roots in a number of centres across the United States – New Orleans, Chicago, Kansas City, Los Angeles – the night time black-and-white pictures of a neon-lit rain-soaked 52nd Street were as potent an image as any motion picture evocation of the City.

Recognising its cultural heritage in a particularly American way, the junction of Fifth Avenue and 52nd Street now bears the sign 'Swing Street', and since the days when the three or four blocks west of there represented the centre of the jazz universe in the 1940s and '50s, jazz has had a permanent place in the cultural life of the Big Apple. For the visitor, New York City is still just about the best place in the world to hear jazz.

Parallel to the jazz scene in the '50s, New York (and on the West Coast, San Francisco) was also the geographical catalyst for the beat generation writers and poets. The triumvirate of Jack Kerouac, Allen Ginsberg and Gregory Corso all lived in Manhattan, even Lawrence Ferlinghetti – who famously became the 'Frisco focus of beat with his City Lights bookshop – first emerged in Greenwich Village before hitting the road west. Nearly 50 years later, the Village is replete with memories of the beat era, from the Café Figaro coffee house on Bleecker Street, where poetry readings were served alongside the espresso and Russian tea, to still-functioning bars and bookshops that were simultaneously social rendezvous and performance venues.

Also largely identified with Greenwich Village was the folk scene. When the young Bob Dylan headed east from his native Minnesota, he was soon a fixture performing on that same circuit of coffee houses, alongside the other young singers like Phil Ochs, Joan Baez and Jack Elliott who constituted the folk 'revival'. Spearheaded by Dylan, this became the launch-pad for folk-rock; one of the enduring images of the era is Dylan with his girlfriend Suze Rotolo walking along Jones Street towards West 4th on the cover of his second album. Although Greenwich Village is no longer the home of a thriving folk scene as such, the City is still host to dynamic folk-rooted music, which isn't stuck in the past, but with artists like the Boggs, Lach and Ladybug Transistor a creative force to be reckoned with.

More so than jazz or folk music of course, rock 'n' roll has been omnipresent in the musical culture of the last half-century. Like jazz, its epicentres have been diverse – Memphis, San Francisco, Seattle – but overall New York has played a bigger part than any of these other places.

From Alan Freed's pioneering radio shows and live concerts at the Brooklyn Paramount, through the doo-wop groups who queued to be auditioned by the songwriters and producers in the Brill Building, to the earliest stirrings of punk in CBGB and Max's Kansas City, it's been a rock 'n' roll town. New wave, no wave, avant-garde rock and hip-hop have all flourished first in NYC, a process most recently manifesting itself in the current boom in records and clubs pinpointed by the success and media coverage of The Strokes and the Yeah Yeah Yeahs, and their contemporaries such as The Walkmen, Longwave and Interpol. It's a vibrant scene spreading out from Manhattan through the boroughs – particularly the new centre, Brooklyn – and across the Hudson to New Jersey.

And this musical history of New York City, first of all in jazz and popular songwriting, then rock 'n' roll, folk-rock, punk, new wave and all the other intertwining genres that were thrown up by the popular music revolution that took place through the 20th century, is very much one that has happened on the street.

For every multimillion dollar record company there are scores of tiny indie labels. For every Madison Square Garden or Giants Stadium there are a thousand small clubs and bar venues. For every superstar there are hundreds of groups, session musicians, singers and songwriters, most struggling to survive but surviving all the same. For every big-time entrepreneur there are the folk who run the clubs and bars and indie labels, day in, day out, week after week, in many cases year after year. They are the people who keep the music scene ticking over, even when times seem bad. It's their life, they can't simply move their investment like the shareholder in a big record corporation, buy shares elsewhere like backing another horse, when the going gets tough.

Just a few such people feature in the pages that follow, a tiny cross section of the grassroots musical life of the city. Plus other individuals who don't have a bearing on the music scene at all – not directly at least – who nevertheless add to the flavour, in many cases a unique New York ambience, that has helped sustain the richness of musical and other creative activity over the years.

They include Rob Sacher, a real mover 'n' shaker on the Lower East Side, whose roster of new names on the stage of his Luna Lounge bar reads like a Who's Who of the cutting edge. And Paul Colby, who has been in the music game for nearly 60 years and is still enjoying himself. There's a quiet Welshman who plays bass guitar on recording sessions down the line – look, no studio – from his Spanish Harlem high-rise, and the ukulele fanatic who runs one of the best little bookstores in the East Village. I talked at length to Lach, the antifolk evangelist who, it turned out, was a fellow Dan Dare fan. That was after spending a lively morning in the company of Johnny Dirt and Jack from Hackensack, manager and owner respectively of the legendary Hell's Kitchen hangout, Rudy's Bar & Grill.

And as well as people there are places. Drinking places, like the piano bar in the Gramercy Park Hotel, 'charmingly seedy' as one reviewer put it but redolent of a more elegant bygone age. Or the Blue Bar of the Algonquin, which, like some grand old dame, has preserved itself much better over the years. Spit-and-sawdust taverns of old – Pete's, McSorley's, Fanelli's – places that vie in the record books for the accolade of the oldest pub in town. And literary watering holes like Chumley's, the White Horse, the Cedar Tavern, where distinguished writers – usually followed closely, it has to be said, by artists and musicians – have famously fallen over, some never to get up again.

And eating places, from the free hot dogs at Rudy's with the best jukebox in town, to the hot Brazilian music and menu at the Union Square Coffee Shop. Live music in restaurants is a far more regular occurrence in New York than in most places, and has been a bread-and-butter (sometimes literally) date in the work diary for generations of musicians. For every 'cocktail lounge' trio happy to play quietly and politely so the customers can hear themselves speak, there have been frustrated jazz and rock players struggling to be heard above the din of busy kitchens, bustling waiters and noisy diners. But, like the man said, it's a gig.

After considerable thought – even toying with the William Burroughs-inspired notion of throwing the various sections of text in the air to see what order they might fall in, letting the laws of chance (and gravity) determine the final structure – I decided to arrange the book on a roughly geographical basis. Though, I should add, I am not attempting to cover every district by any means – just those where my brief dictated and my mission took me. That way, for the potential visitor and armchair tourist alike, there's a 'neighbourhood' feel that reflects, I hope, the sheer diversity of New York City. It's a diversity sometimes apparent block by block, a variety of culture that's mirrored in the rich mix of its music.

Along the way, between talking to people and listening to music, I've stopped and stared here, reflected on some afterthought there, dug into a little history somewhere else. So don't expect a neat guide book or street-by-street walking tour. *Waking Up In New York City* can be as entertaining, diverting and fulfilling as you want to make it. Try it yourself, and enjoy!

1 Spanish Harlem Afternoon

One of the great joys of Manhattan is its shape, from which has evolved possibly the easiest-to-handle big city transport system in the world. The north-to-south, east-to-west grid pattern of the streets north of Houston Street in the Village has defined a similarly simple arrangement of subway lines and bus routes extending right down to the southernmost tip at Battery Park.

Even parts of the City you've never visited before are as easy to find as familiar locations. Streamlined ticketing like the electronic Metrocard – anywhere on the system for two dollars (£1.25) a ride, including change of buses – makes life even easier, especially for the visitor. Buy, say, a $20 (£12.50) card and, when it's nearing its limit, top it up at a machine in the subway. When you come back to NYC six months, a year later, it's still valid, just top it up some more. Hey, (after a London transport infrastructure that seems to get worse rather than better) public transport can be fun to use.

After years, and many occasions, of visiting New York, until recently I had never been further north than East 91st Street and Fifth Avenue, (visiting the always exciting Cooper-Hewitt Design Museum), save for the view from a railway train heading out from Penn Station through the Bronx on the way to Boston. So when I contacted an old friend and musical colleague of over 30 years ago and he invited me to his apartment in Spanish Harlem up on East 106th Street, this was new territory.

Although only a handful of blocks from the 'Museum Mile' section of Fifth Avenue running along the east side of Central Park (which takes in the Metropolitan, the Guggenheim, the Cooper-Hewitt and the Jewish

Museum on the way) the junction of East 106th and Third Avenue might as well have been in a different city. The bus ride along Third from Astor Place in the East Village passes through increasingly grand neighbourhoods on the Upper East Side and fashionable Yorkville up in the Nineties, before the landscape changes fairly abruptly around 98th, 99th, and you are suddenly in *el barrio*, the Hispanic 'hood known as Spanish Harlem.

Indeed, the northernmost of the string of museums along Fifth Avenue, up between 104th and 105th Streets, is El Museo del Barrio, dedicated to the work of Latino artists in the US and Latin American art generally, taking its name from the district, *barrio,* referring to any Spanish-speaking quarter in American cities.

I've come to visit Percy Jones, a Welsh-born bass player who has lived in New York for 25 years or so. He lives in a housing project on 106th, just a block or two from where I alight from the bus, greeting me at the door of his apartment after I've negotiated a creaking lift, his dog Sparky barking ferociously at strangers.

Percy shares his home with his wife of all those years, Joyce Francis, a black American, born and bred in Harlem, not far from where we are now. Joyce makes amazing jewellery, handbags and even furniture out of sculpted acrylic, which she sells through smart retail outlets and has had exhibited in various exhibitions and galleries. Her 'workbench', machines and all, is the kitchen table.

Joyce shows me some of her work, the hand-carved acrylic having the quality of fine glass – or even a strange work of nature, an organic feel in an ostensibly 'futuristic' medium. Some of her pieces have asymmetrical lines or flowing curves, hand-formed with the use of heat. Her technique involves carving figurative motifs into the acrylic, then either tinting it with delicate crystalline tones, painting it, or leaving it clear or opaque. She explains, 'At times, the transparency of the acrylic gives it the appearance of an aqueous suspension of the carved images. I love this.'

The results are certainly remarkable, and she's been acknowledged in a number of galleries and museums in America, Scandinavia and even at the Victoria and Albert Museum in London, where one of her handbags is now in the permanent collection. And although all her work, from trinket-size brooches to monumental sculptures, is infused with the same passion, she has a particular fondness for the 'costume' items, the jewellery, purses and bags: 'The idea of a woman owning a portable, wearable legend that brings her pleasure is really exciting'.

Percy practises and creates his music, and even puts down tracks for records, in his cramped adjoining 'studio' space, which – he's an electronics freak, always has been – doubles as a ham-radio base. Although he plays live gigs with his trio Tunnels, the session work that has subsidised his income for many years is being done as often as not 'down the line'; the journey to some downtown studio to lay down maybe one track on someone's album giving way more and more to Percy playing it at home, the bass track whizzing electronically to be mixed with the rest in Chicago, LA, wherever. Such is technology – but like I said, he's always been into that sort of stuff.

I first met Percy Jones in the late 1960s when he was still studying electronic engineering at Liverpool University. The late poet – and dear friend – Adrian Henri, myself and others were putting together a poetry/rock outfit, which became known as The Liverpool Scene. The guitarist Andy Roberts, who was also at the University at the time, mentioned a bass guitarist he'd been playing with in a student band called The Trip (very psychedelic!) and suggested we give him a try.

From the start his style was unique, and when he moved to the unconventional fretless bass guitar – inspired by the double bass still played by most of his jazz idols, particularly Charles Mingus – the technique and originality he exhibited, even in the limited musical circumstances of our 'mixed-media' experiments, was nothing short of sensational. By the time the band split in 1970, it was clear Percy was looking to explore new musical frontiers; he wasn't sure what that might be, but certainly jazz-rock and the emerging 'fusion' scene were the direction in which his music was leaning, and a move to London the direction he had to take to make it possible.

He moved to the unlikely suburb of Beckenham, purely because he had a place to stay there, where fortuitously the pianist/composer Keith Tippett and his vocalist wife Julie (*née* Driscoll) also resided.

'That was just somewhere where I managed to find somewhere to live, you know, through a contact, somebody I'd met, who said, "I can hook you up with an apartment where I live in Beckenham." So I moved to Beckenham, with a place to live there, and I was working on a building site, I was just surviving in Beckenham.

'And I met some of the local musicians there, actually Keith Tippett was living there, so I met him and Julie, got to know them pretty well…and one of them was Robin Lumley, and he said, "We've got this get-together" – I think it was on a Wednesday night – "in a rehearsal hall in Clapham, a bunch of us just get together and jam, you know, wanna come along?" So I went along and played…it turned into a regular Wednesday night session, you know, we'd all get together and play, and it was fun.'

The ensuing collaboration resulted in a short-lived liaison with Island Records, before the eventual line-up ended up on Charisma Records – with Phil Collins on drums – as Brand X.

'One day, one of the guys comes in and says, "I've hooked up an audition at Island Records," and we all started laughing, but he'd hooked it up, so the following day we went to Island and played for these two A&R guys, I think Richard Williams was one of them, and we didn't really have any tunes, it was just like mostly improvising…I was bowing the bass, using the wah wah pedal…we didn't take it seriously and we'd been drinking, everybody was half smashed, and Richard Williams loved it, and they signed us up.

'Anyway, to make a long story short, we were with Island for – it can't have been more than a year – and we recorded a record for them, which had vocals on it, and it was sort of like a below-Average White Band type thing, and we didn't like it, we weren't very happy with it, we asked [Island boss] Chris Blackwell if we could can that one and do another one that was all instrumental, and he said okay.

'We changed the line-up a little bit, we changed drummers, and that's when Phil Collins joined, and we did another record, which was all instrumental, which we really liked but Chris Blackwell didn't. So Island dumped us. Luckily Charisma picked us up, and took on the new record that Island had rejected, and that was the first Brand X record.'

Collins, who at the time led a parallel existence with Genesis after the departure of Peter Gabriel, reckoned the band to be second only to Weather Report in the jazz-rock stakes, and the quartet, completed by Lumley on keyboards and Atomic Rooster's John Goodsall on guitar (for whom, like Collins, it was initially a side-project) became one of the most commercially successful British jazz-rock groups of that era. As far as Jones recalls, it all came as a bit of a surprise: '…and then we started touring, making more dough. It was a pretty weird start, I mean I'm glad it worked that way, but it was unexpected.'

Their records, for what was admittedly a niche audience, did well. After their 1976 debut *Unorthodox Behaviour*, 1977's *Livestock* did even better and *Moroccan Roll* the same year hit the lower 30s in the UK album chart. For a while, they were sort of what you'd call big.

'Yeah, but it was a limited audience, a specific audience, and we ended up playing more in this country than we did in England. Because in England it would always be like one nighters, we'd go to Manchester, do a gig, a couple of weeks later there'd be a gig in Scotland, you know, one-off things, whereas over here we'd do tours, a couple of tours a year, ten weeks solid. So it seemed that we were more accepted here than there, which was odd because the music we were playing was sort of jazz-rock, it was like we were taking coals to Newcastle.

'And that's why I moved here, because I was working more here, and then I met my wife, who is a native, you know she's from Harlem, so I just decided to move here. Another reason is that I like the diversity here and you can find musicians that can pretty much play any style of music. All the drummers that we used, with the exception of Phil Collins, were from over here. As you know, I've got a soft spot for jazz and most of the jazz people are here also.

'That was…I think it was in 1978, and Brand X was still pretty active. And then Brand X broke up in 1980 because the money stopped coming in. And we were so spread out, I was living here, John Goodsall was living in LA…'

Percy was the only member of the band actually living in New York: 'Yeah, John had moved to LA, so we were all spread out, and we never got any royalties, nobody had any money really to speak of, so we couldn't under our own steam get in one place to play together, you know? So it just sort of folded up.

'But since then we've put it back together as a trio on and off, you know, Goodsall, me and Lumley, sporadically until '97, and then I left…'

After that Percy exploited his already well-established reputation as a session player, a reputation that went back to his days on the London scene after moving from Liverpool.

'The session thing over the years has gotten less and less. The most sessions I ever did was when I came to London in the late '70s, I used to do quite a bit. You always got paid union scale and it's pretty good money… But yeah, I still get calls for sessions but it's always like, "We'll give you a hundred bucks [£65] if you play on this track," whereas before it was always scale. But it rolled off over the years.

'Make a living from music? On and off. I'd say half, half the time I can't make a living from making music. I supplement it by working for Joyce on her jewellery. It's up and down, I get a job, get nice, good pay, and then there's nothing for a couple of months…'

And, like in so many other walks of life, the new technology has resulted in a lot more home-based activity:

'What is happening now, which is interesting, is with the technology that's around, I can do stuff at home. For example, there's an Irish singer, Cora Simms, she's on *Tubular Bells* actually, a really good singer. I just did a few tracks for her, and then yesterday I got a call from a band in Chicago to do a bunch of tracks, the same way, sort of doing it at home, which is great, you can take your time. You know when you're in a studio it's so many dollars an hour and budgets and watching the clock, whereas at home you just go at your own pace. So that method of doing things is kind of picking up actually, which I'm happy about. The straight-up session thing of being called into a studio has been on the decline.'

There have always been the live outfits as well, of course, the core to any musician's activity, though not necessarily the most regular:

'In the early '80s I played with a few different outfits, one was a band called Noise 'R' Us that [CBGB owner] Hilly Kristal probably remembers, we played a lot at CB's…and they had to change the name to Powernoise because of Toys 'R' Us. Toys 'R' Us were going to sue them, some sort of legal problem…'

Percy was involved in several such groups before putting together the current trio, Tunnels, which operates on an admittedly occasional basis.

With a line-up completed by Marc Wagnon on vibes and drummer Frank Katz, since 1992 they have been the platform for Percy's singular style of sonic exploration, anchoring as it does in his faultless rhythmic pulse at the ultra-low end of his instrument, Wagnon's compositional as well as improvisational skills, and Katz's hothouse percussion. They made their debut record-wise with a self-titled album in 1994, and their latest release *Progressivity* features as guest, among others, old Brand X colleague John Goodsall.

'Originally it was very occasional. That started back in the early '90s actually and it was really sporadic: we'd get a gig somewhere and then nothing for six weeks and then another gig. It was so intermittent everybody would forget the tunes. You'd get a gig, and you'd start that gig getting the rust off, remembering the arrangements. And if we had a so-called tour, it would be like three dates, three or four dates, and by the fourth one it'd be just burning and we'd be really starting to play well…then we wouldn't get another for weeks.

'Although it's getting more regular now… We tried to jack it up to get it more active, and we're gigging more than we've ever done. We're working pretty hard to play more regularly, in fact February, March and April we did a whole bunch of gigs…down through North Carolina, Nashville… It was interesting in Nashville, 'cos this band would open for us, you know these local guys, really into jazz, but they did country studio work – that's where they made their bread, you know – but jazz was their first love.

'The guitar player who was on the first Tunnels record, Van Manakas, he lives and works in Nashville, and he's doing a lot of stuff. I heard a record he's just done, and I was amazed that he could play like that. He was doing all this sort of country stuff, and somebody put it on in the van when we were driving, and I didn't know it was him and I said, "Who's this good guitar player?"

'And they said, "It's Van," and I was amazed, I didn't know he could play like that…'

Session work notwithstanding, the live music scene is of constant concern. I comment that looking down the venue lists in the New York press – and elsewhere – the scene in the US appears to be a lot healthier than in London.

'Well here, the club thing is tough because usually you get a percentage at the door, so unless there's a good turnout you don't make any money, you cover your expenses, and that's it. But I'm sort of in communication with some musicians in England and it sounded like over there it was worse.

'The last time I was in London was the summer of '97. It was the last time I played with Brand X: it was terrible, absolutely terrible. The first gig was at the Jazz Café, which was good, that was a good turnout, and I think the next night we were in Oxford, and it was like ten people or something. All the dates were like that, I mean sometimes 30 or 40. Then we went down to Italy and it completely changed: we played in this big club in Rome and it was packed. But that was the first time I'd played in England in 20 years or more and it'll probably be the last, I mean it was so disappointing.'

Sparky, the black-and-white Alsatian/Doberman mongrel whose bark is worse than his bite, wants to go walkies. Percy's regular route is straight west along 106th to where it meets the top end of the Park. Bidding Joyce goodbye, we hit the street.

It's a tough-looking neighbourhood, there's no question about that, but Percy's quick to point out that it used to be a lot worse when he first moved here from the more comfortable environment of Park Slope, Brooklyn.

'When I first came here [the US] we lived in Brooklyn, Park Slope, a really nice building, and it was a nice area. Not knowing how the New York thing works, we signed a one-year lease, and after a year the rent went up, so then we moved to where we are now…'

An injection of civic money and private investment in the '90s started to put the area on its feet at last, though Percy's big fear (and that of most residents and civic leaders) is that in the current political climate, with the wind-down of public funding, things are being turned round to how it was in the 'bad old days'.

'I think it reached a low point in the early '90s, then through to the later '90s it [civic money] started to trickle down. It's a lot better: there are more cops on the street now, that sort of thing, you feel safer...'

Nevertheless, Percy's been mugged almost on his doorstep, and admits there's a certain antagonism from some individuals (albeit a minority) on the street because of his colour, and, inevitably, the fact his wife is black. But, after all these years, this is his patch, which he refers to like the local that he is, as 'the *barrio*'.

'It's way better than it was, but it's not completely OK...like last night I heard "bam, bam, bam" about one o'clock, so I turned the scanner on. I have a scanner so I can listen to the cops, so if I hear shooting I always turn it on to see where it is. It'll say, "Shots fired, 112th Street and First"...but yeah, it's a lot better than it was about six years ago.'

We enter Central Park just four blocks from its northernmost point, with the Harlem Meer lake to our right, beyond which you can see the skyline of Harlem proper along Central Park North, the parkside extension of East 110th Street. Percy tells me how a day or so earlier he and Sparky witnessed an NYPD helicopter fishing a guy's body out of the water – where nobody swims, it seems – after he got into trouble and drowned.

The Park here is less well-kept, perhaps, than further south where the horse-drawn buggies glide by; it's certainly more 'natural', less landscaped, for that. For Percy, it's a welcome bit of countryside. Though eschewing London, he still visits his hometown and family in rural Wales every year, still drinking in the local pub with guys he's known since schooldays.

It would be tempting to say he's a country boy at heart, but I suspect not. His heart's always been in his music and wherever that was going to take him. In Percy's case – for not just one but a number of reasons, like with any of the millions of immigrants who have become part of the fabric of the City – it became clear that that destination was New York a long time ago.

2 Midtown Rhapsody

A sound-and-picture image of New York that for ever sticks in the mind is the opening sequence of Woody Allen's 1978 movie *Manhattan* – described by one critic as Allen's 'glorious love letter to the city that he was born to make films about'. Immaculate black-and-white images of the City are crucially set against a soundtrack of George Gershwin's iconic 'Rhapsody In Blue'.

The 16-minute Gershwin piece, written in the pre-Depression jazz-age years of the early 1920s, is the perfect musical paean to the ultimate big city. It evokes a New York that was literally new, a thoroughly modern Manhattan of Art Deco elegance and neon optimism, a bustling, machine-driven metropolis where anything seemed possible and more shining buildings redefined the skyline every day.

From the opening clarinet glissando to the closing strident exchanges between piano and orchestra, it's the Manhattan of Times Square theaterland and Grand Central Station, Fifth Avenue shops and smart hotels overlooking the Park. It's the Manhattan of midtown.

GOTHAM GRAND, GOTHAM GOTHIC

Back when Gershwin was penning his masterpiece, Grand Central Station had just been completed, a cathedral-like building of epic proportions with a vast concourse that functioned as a public space in its own right. Indeed, in the 1940s there was a radio series called *Grand Central* featuring stories from the 'thousand dramas daily' supposedly played out there.

The building was almost doomed for demolition in the 1970s, before a Supreme Court intervention saved it, but since then it's been refurbished to its former glory, the imposing concourse roof once more a bright blue with its 'starry sky' of golden astrological decorations.

The huge arched causeways taking you down to a complex of shops and cafés reveal another institution that has survived, the Grand Central Oyster Bar, where locals throng at lunchtimes for its dizzying array of seafood delights – despite the cavernous ceilings, which make conversation a rowdy, but very New York, affair.

Running along the south side of Grand Central Terminal, which is sprawled across an intricate system of flyovers and tunnels that interface with Park Avenue, is 42nd Street. One block east to Lexington Avenue and you're standing right underneath the Chrysler Building. And I mean underneath.

When I talked of Grand Central being 'cathedral-like', I was referring to the awesome interior more than the outside; with the Chrysler it's just the reverse. There's public access to the amazing Deco lobby, with those ornate faux-Egyptian elevator gates beloved of hotels and department stores of that period, but the rest of the building is for the use of the office dwellers who work there. And the folk (no doubt with other things on their mind), among them an old friend of mine, who used to visit a dentist who had his surgery up on the top floor.

But it's when you stop and gaze up at the Chrysler – yeah, OK, I know they say the way to recognise a visitor in New York is that they're the ones looking up all the time – the sense of awe is akin to that inspired by the great European churches of old; and of course in the latter case that was the whole point. I'm not a religious person, in fact the interiors of most of those dark, musty temples I just find scary – and that was probably the point as well – but stand outside Cologne Cathedral and few would fail to be moved by the sheer size, combined with a mind-boggling attention to detail on a superhuman scale.

And it's that carefully crafted ornamentation, the fine detail of which can never be seen from the ground – which is where most will ever see the building from – that old cathedrals have in common with the Chrysler and other older, 'Gothic'-ornamented skyscrapers, in the City. The Chrysler, designed by William Van Alen as an evocation of the automobile age in the late 1920s, has stainless steel 'gargoyles' and a 'crown' fashioned to represent hub caps, which can only be really appreciated by someone leaning out of an office window in the building itself or from a passing helicopter. Still, that's better than any opportunity the good citizens of Cologne had, to see the finer points of *their* city's pride and joy when it was first built.

New York, perhaps surprisingly, has some *real* Gothic – well, 19th-century Gothic Revival – architecture in its midst, most notable of all being, appropriately, an actual cathedral. It's St Patrick's, on Fifth Avenue, right opposite the Art Deco grandeur of the Rockefeller Center shops and office complex. Once the dominant structure on this part of Fifth – it's still the biggest Catholic cathedral in the United States – over the years its twin steeples have become overshadowed by the skyscrapers surrounding it, an example of stylistic juxtaposition that's extreme even by Manhattan standards.

SWING STREET

Going west along 42nd, until recently, it was apparent what the street had become famous for over the past few decades: sleaze. Through to Times Square at Broadway and beyond, it was strip joint after porn cinema after 'adult' video store. Likewise with Times Square itself, that neon-flash junction of Broadway and Seventh Avenue between 42nd and 44th Streets, until the Mayor Giuliani-inspired 'clean up' in the 1990s. It was a much-needed reform that many New Yorkers nevertheless felt went too far, losing some of the district's essential character along the way.

In addition to their numbered designation, sections of streets and avenues across Manhattan have been given names as well. Not in order to confuse taxi drivers, pedestrians or postmen – 'officially' the number system rules – but to honour some person, event or other aspect associated with that part of the thoroughfare.

So it is that at the junction of Fifth Avenue, the sign for West 52nd Street reads 'Swing Street'. During and just after World War II, that section of 52nd from Fifth through to Seventh Avenue was the hotbed of all that was new and happening in jazz. Known simply as 'The Street' to the musicians who worked the clubs there, it was the epicentre of the bebop revolution being spearheaded by Dizzy Gillespie, Charlie ('Bird') Parker and their contemporaries. After-dark pictures taken at the time look like there was nothing else there but jazz clubs, so numerous are the illuminated signs. In their celebrated book of jazz interviews *Hear Me Talkin' To Ya*, first published in 1955, Nat Shapiro and Nat Hentoff spoke to pianist Billy Taylor about working on 52nd Street in the early '40s.

'In 1943, I remember the Deuces, the Downbeat, the Onyx, the Famous Door, Kelly's Stable, and the Hickory House... The big three draws on The Street then were Art Tatum, Coleman Hawkins and Billie Holiday. And things were flexible for musicians on The Street. Like Don Byas might have an engagement at the Three Dueces as a leader, and then he'd go next door to the Downbeat as a sideman with Coleman Hawkins.'

Furious informal 'cutting sessions' would take place with musicians literally competing on stage, and this potent atmosphere helped give birth to the new music that was being forged all around.

It's a far, far cry from that now, the Swing Street sign the only indication that this was once the centre of the jazz universe, though one name appears on 52nd Street that's been there since the 1930s: Roseland Ballroom, over between Broadway and Eighth Avenue. Featured in the 1977 Merchant-Ivory movie *Roseland*, which told of ageing characters who returned to the tea-dance atmosphere of their long-lost youth, the ballroom did indeed stage old-fashioned ballroom dancing events way after they were no longer regularly viable. Still does, in fact, but also functions as a rock-music venue, among other things.

I visited Roseland a few years back, its big once-inviting frontage somewhat dilapidated, peeling posters and spray-can graffiti indicative of its latter-day role as a fairly rough and ready rock venue, though like many places of late it's since undergone a facelift. Bob Dylan was headlining that night, in front of a capacity crowd in the sprawling seen-better-days dance hall. The support act, confident and sassy-looking though few had heard of her, was a new female singer by the name of Sheryl Crow.

These days Roseland advertises itself as an all-round venue, available for hire for all sorts of events. Recent functions there have included private weddings, fashion shows (Versace, no less), even a tattoo artists' convention! And, naturally, rock 'n' roll features heavily, with names like Hootie And The Blowfish, Liz Phair and those cutting-edge chart-punks from Detroit, The White Stripes.

A TIME STOOD STILL

Like Roseland, Grand Central and Times Square, much of New York has undergone refurbishment, restoration and general smartening up in recent years, and by and large this is no bad thing. It's certainly preferable to the orgy of destruction that swept the City in the '60s and '70s, when 'planners' laid waste to anything they could swing a wrecking ball at.

One place that has benefited from the caring touch of some loving restoration, while retaining its old Manhattan charm with confidence over the decades, is the Algonquin.

Probably the City's most famous literary landmark, this West 44th Street hotel, which first opened for business in 1902, gained its fame when a group of writers met in June 1919 for a luncheon to welcome Aleck Woollcott, the drama critic for the *New York Times*, back from World War I. Among his friends were newspaper columnist Franklin P Adams, the future publisher of *The New Yorker* Harold Ross, and the famed journalist Dorothy Parker, who was the drama critic at *Vanity Fair* at the time.

The much-quoted Parker was the catalyst for what very quickly became known as the Round Table group, so named because they met regularly at a round table in the hotel's Rose Room. It soon became the most celebrated literary gathering in American letters, before or since, and for ten years the eminent journalists, magazine editors and critics – plus actors and assorted hangers-on – would rule the landscape of the New York literati during Prohibition. They would meet in the Rose Room for long, liquid lunches, followed some nights by a poker game upstairs in one of their rooms.

Staying at, or just visiting, the 'Gonk' (as it was affectionately known by the Round Tablers and generations since) is to step into a living museum of a New York otherwise long gone. The grand Lobby exudes an almost-forgotten quiet-paced elegance, the Oak Room is still host to cabaret a couple of times a week, the Rose Room is there with its literary ghosts. And the hotel cat snoozes on the reception desk.

And right next door, adjoining the Lobby but also opening onto the street, the hotel's famed Blue Bar – reputed to serve the finest Bloody Mary in New York City – further evokes that Manhattan of yesteryear. The jukebox always seems to be playing Sinatra – the classic 1950s sides of course, none of your 'New York, New York' or 'My Way' showbiz stuff – while the veteran barmen move as if time has stood still, which for them it probably has. Let's just say you don't come in here for a quick drink.

LAST DIVE IN THE KITCHEN

It's a cliché to say that New York is a city of contrasts, but there's no bigger contrast imaginable than taking a walk from the Blue Bar, straight over Sixth Avenue, Times Square and so on until you hit Ninth Avenue, and Rudy's Bar & Grill. It's got a great jukebox, has changed little over the years and is a monument to an all-but-extinct aspect of New York life. But there any remote similarity with the Blue Bar and its parent establishment ends. Rudy's is a surviving example of another, quite different, Manhattan institution, the neighbourhood dive bar.

I first came across Rudy's – or at least Rudy's reputation – via my son, who in turn had heard it mentioned on a local London radio station. Apparently it was acknowledged as having the best jukebox in New York City: good enough reason to check it out further. Digging deeper, I found various references to its famed free hot dogs, and the 'five-cent [3p] chicken dinner': a hard-boiled egg! The hot dogs are still free, the chicken dinner, alas, a thing of the past.

When you hit the junction of 44th Street and Ninth, you can't miss Rudy's; just look for the 2m (6ft) smiling pig standing on the sidewalk. Or, as the bar's own website puts it: 'The neon sign and the giant swine'. He's known as Baron Von Swine to regulars, the 'loquacious locals and colourful comrades' that make up Rudy's core clientele.

It's a classic dive joint, with the bar running down one side, the inevitable TV set flickering silently and a couple of booths opposite, leaving room for drinkers to sit at the bar itself or cram into the space between. The famous jukebox is at the end of the room; beyond that there's a door leading to a 'garden' area. The selection of music on the '80s-vintage 'box is eclectic, the only constant being quality. Billie Holiday, The Beatles, Cab Calloway, Jimi Hendrix; English punk and New York funk, jazz, country and lots of rhythm and blues.

The first time I visited Rudy's I got the life story of the old guy standing next to me in about five minutes flat, while vintage Count Basie roared in the background. It was five in the afternoon, he said he'd been there all day and was going home to 'make way for the young crowd' that took over at six. The second time, six months later, it was ten at night, full of that young crowd, Hendrix on the 'box. My wife, asking if they had a Chardonnay, was told in no uncertain terms that they sold two kinds of wine, white and red. It's that kind of place.

Rudy's prides itself on being part of the cultural fabric of Hell's Kitchen, the tough West Side area that lies between Eighth Avenue and the Hudson River, from 34th Street up to 57th. One of the melting-pot districts of New York during its 19th-century evolution, with immigrants of every colour and creed thronging its streets and tenements, the area was synonymous with the tougher side of Manhattan life from the start. Small wonder Leonard Bernstein set West Side Story right there.

Rudy's is run by a larger-than-life character who goes by the name of Johnny Dirt, real name John Schroeder, and owned by an equally engaging – and genial – individual, Jack Earl, who Schroeder refers to as 'Jack from Hackensack'.

As soon as we meet, before repairing to the garden to talk, Johnny introduces me to a couple of locals propping up the mid-morning bar. One is in his 90s, an ex-longshoreman who'd worked the nearby docks all his life, the other a would-be actor who confesses that after having a two-word speaking role opposite Paul Newman in The Hustler in 1961 his career has been 'downhill ever since'.

Johnny Dirt has only actually been running the place for five years or so, but has been around the New York club and bar scene since the early punk days at CBGB and Max's Kansas City.

'I had a nightclub in New Jersey, the Purple Grotto, which to me was the most famous club going. I booked 5,000 bands, all original, that was the only thing that made it different. And anyone who came to me, I gave them a booking, I didn't care how good they were, how bad they were, it didn't fucking matter. But it had to be original. They'd say, "How'd we do, Johnny?"

'I'd say, "Yeah, you did great, man, you gotta go back into the garage, go down to your basement, stroke it up on that guitar, beat them drums, come back and you can have a booking. If you stay together, you'll get better together."

'I've been running the place four or five years, but I've been coming in here for 30, 40 years. I don't own Rudy's Bar, the guy who owns Rudy's Bar, you should talk to him, he could be the most interesting character you ever met in your life. Jack from Hackensack. He spent 50 years on the high seas, he was a head engineer for Exon, their oldest employee, he's been around the world more times than anybody I know, he's been to every country, 50 years at it.'

Before long, Jack Earl, a stocky guy with what you would call a well-lived-in face, arrives from an office upstairs where he'd been meeting with Johnny earlier. He tells me how he took over the bar about 20 years ago, from the German family who had run it for three generations.

'The Rudy family got run out of Germany in the early '30s or mid '30s and they came over here, and in those days in the Land of the Free, the Home of the Brave, you couldn't have a bottle of beer because we had Prohibition. So they ran this place here as a speakeasy. So it's been a bar, I guess, since the mid '30s or early '30s. But it became legal in the mid '30s when you could legally buy a bottle of beer. It's been Rudy's ever since; actually the Rudy family have been here for three generations. But the third generation, they got a better education, and they moved onto something bigger and better. And that's where I came in.'

He explains how Rudy's is now one of the last of the 'neighbourhood' bars that helped give New York its character.

'This is probably the last of what you would call a neighbourhood bar in midtown Manhattan. 'Cos there's not very many neighbourhood bars left. And we have so many people coming into here, just like the former owner, they've been here for three generations, I would imagine four, but I don't know…

'Some of these buildings here in this street were here during the Civil War, between 1860 and 1865. I used to have a bar on 48th Street, just off Broadway, and they say during the Civil War Abraham Lincoln stayed there. During the Civil War the Italian Embassy was located at 48th and 8th Avenue I think. Later it became a very famous restaurant there, Mama Leoni. But some of the buildings in the area might be 150 years old.'

The area was notorious as a 'tough' neighbourhood, hence its nickname Hell's Kitchen, with a history bathed in a certain amount of blood and conflict, not unlike the area now part of Chinatown, which was the setting for Martin Scorsese's *Gangs Of New York*.

'It was so rough, in the 1830s to 1850s when they had an awful lot of Irish immigrants coming to this country, and it was just like hell. The Irish were beating one another up, and if you weren't careful you got beat up just because you were here. So it was hell. And the higher-class people were living on the east side of town, and it was just like a small town down south where the whites lived on one side of the street and the blacks on the other… The good quality people lived east of Broadway, and over here…over here were the immigrants, and the gangsters with the pimps, the whores, the drug dealers, the horse thieves. The island had been sort of divided like that since the early 1800s from what I understand.'

The bar is on the edge of the Theater District. Were some of the regulars theatre people?

'We really don't get actors, we get people who call themselves actors and actresses, but they are really bartenders and barmaids who are struggling. That doesn't mean that some of 'em haven't made it to the top, cos some of 'em have. But most of them are really not actors and actresses, they're barmaids and bartenders, and waiters.'

Jack was conscious of the fact that the area, and so to some extent the bar's regular customers, had changed over the years.

'I would say during the war, in the '40s, the majority of people that would come to this bar and other bars in this area were mainly longshoremen, stevedores, seamen and people who did repairs on ships.

Right across the river was a shipyard called Todd Shipyards. So they built ships a 15-minute ride over the bridge, and there was an awful lot of shipyard workers in those days. Now most of the people who drink here live in the area.'

I mentioned the fact that the crowd in the bar seemed to get visibly 'younger' in the evening.

'The people who are here in the daytime are retired people, and when the sun goes down they wanna go home and watch TV, they wanna hear the late news, the ball scores and what have you, they're already drank out, and a new shift comes in, a younger shift that get off work at five o'clock… If they're young people, they got good livers, means they can drink more. The old farts that are hanging around here that are retired, their livers are half shot already, they been drinking for 30, 40 years, like myself!'

Like the millions of residents that have adopted New York (or its environs, he lives in Hackensack, New Jersey) as their home, not just immigrants to the US but out-of-towners like himself, Jack is as proud of the City as a true native.

'It's a great place to be. I'm originally from Chicago, I came to this area as a teenager, but I ain't never going back to Chicago. It has its advantages, the greatest transportation system in the world. You wanna go anywhere, you walk outside, put your hand up, you get a taxi, or you walk half a block and you can get a subway. You can go anywhere in the City and the price is right.

Two dollars (£1.25) anywhere…

'Two dollars [£1.25]? When I was a kid, it was five cents [3p]…inflation, huh?

'You can go from north of the Bronx, all the way to Coney Island, you can ride all day, you don't have to get off, you can get right back too, for the same price.

'When I was a kid it was five cents. If you were unfortunate enough not to have a place to sleep and you had five cents, you could get on the subway, and you rode all night, and after about eight hours on the subway you were sober enough, then you went out looking for a job in the morning, but you didn't have to worry about a place to sleep, you could sleep back on the subway, in fact someone wrote a book one time, *Subways Are For Sleeping.*

'And when you were broke and didn't have any money, even five cents to get in the subway, if you went to the ticket taker at the counter and said, "Hey look, I'm broke, I haven't got a nickel," she'd let you slip underneath the turnstile. I never was that bad off, but I knew people who were. Those struggling young actors and actresses that didn't quite make it, they slept on the subway.'

I don't know who wrote the blurb for Rudy's website, but it glows with a poetry that sums up the place and its uniqueness:

'The clientele is as diverse as the neighbourhood and the city of which it is part: 80-year-old Hell's Kitchen veterans raise glasses with the next generation of locals, city-spanning saunterers, international interlopers, journalists, performers, dreamers and ramblers. Is the guy sitting next to you an artist, a poet, or just a drunk? You never know at Rudy's!

'Listen to the streets, and you'll hear the scrape of utensils sharpening, the clink and clank of pots and pans over an open flame – and you'll know: the chef is getting ready, because something's cooking in Hell's Kitchen.'

3 Good Morning Chelsea

Although there are parallels between London's Chelsea, where I live, and the New York district of the same name – in terms of a bohemian tradition that goes back to the 19th century and a contemporary trendiness that makes it a smart location these days – physically it couldn't look more different.

Situated west of Fifth Avenue between 14th and 29th Streets, the dilapidated-looking grid of tenements and warehouses reflects a seedy past. It never became the fashionable area some thought it might at the end of the 19th century, when it was briefly the focus for a bohemian influx because of its proximity to the theatrical district.

It soon lost out in this respect to the nearby Greenwich Village, and for years the area was dominated – like Hell's Kitchen, its neighbour to the north – by warehouses, slaughterhouses, the elevated railway and a poor working class, all reflecting its proximity to the Hudson River docks.

Of late, however, the area has taken on a new lease of life, initially as a centre for artists, echoing that same dynamic that has turned other run-down warehouse districts first into low-rent art colonies then in turn into fashionable areas full of galleries, restaurants, 'desirable' dwellings and prices that reflect their new-found image. Think East Village, Lower East Side, the Bowery, Brooklyn.

At the same time, it still looks generally down-at-heel for vast stretches of Sixth, Seventh, Eighth…right over to Eleventh Avenue, despite smart townhouses and refurbed terraces giving an air of recently renovated grandness to the otherwise mean streets in between.

SHOP TILL YOU BOP

In fact, they don't look much meaner early on a Saturday or Sunday morning than the windswept stretch of Sixth Avenue between West 24th and 26th Streets, where you'll find one of the best flea markets in the City. The Annex Antiques Fair & Market has been attracting bargain-hunters for years now, ranging from the needy looking for some essential household item to the affluent willing to pay pumped-up prices for junky bric-a-brac from a clued-in dealer.

And these days, most of the dealers seem a lot more clued-in than they used to be. There were always the 'trade' characters of course, who knew the prices were already beginning to escalate on items like Deco pottery or vintage clothing, but you could still pick up old vinyl, comics, magazines, books and pure trash for small change.

It was only five or six years ago, in the two-floor indoor 'Garage' market nearby, that I came across two mint-condition copies of the original 1976 *Punk* magazine – Numbers 1 and 4 – which chronicled the local scene back when Debbie Harry was a regular favourite at CBGB's, described in its pages as 'the sexiest chick on the New York underground rock scene'. They cost me a couple of dollars each. Similar finds of late would run to $10 (£6), $15 (£10) at least, and this is a flea market, not a collectors' shop, where the price tag might be double again.

Wandering round is always great fun, the Garage especially good for more unusual items. You might just be looking for an old birdcage or vintage Mickey Mouse money box, some 1930s sheet music or a copy of a Bettie Page pin-up magazine; whatever, you're as likely to find it here as anywhere, and a lot cheaper.

Just a short walk away along West 26th Street, between Seventh and Eighth, shopping of a very different kind takes place, in what looks like an almost secret location. Number 236 is one of those huge warehouse-type blocks that characterise the area, and getting to Room 804 involves using an entryphone to announce your presence downstairs. Once up there, sturdy metal doors open to welcome you to – no, not the Manhattan branch of Fort Knox, or some nefarious drug dealership – but a record shop. To be more precise, the best jazz record shop in New York City.

The Jazz Record Center has been functioning as both a store and mail-order facility since the early 1980s, and prides itself on a second-to-none selection of old and rare vinyl and CDs or, as its business card blurb puts it: 'Jazz and jazz-related recordings of all styles and speeds' – plus books, magazines, posters and videos, all pertaining to jazz.

The interior of the store makes no concessions to in-shop niceties; instead, there is rack after rack, shelf after shelf, of recordings by every conceivable name in the history of jazz, from blues to bop, New Orleans to new wave. The dedicated fan could spend several days here, without seeing the light of the sun, content on thumbing through tens of thousands of albums.

The center's website lists the latest acquisitions – part of the business is to buy whole collections from those willing to part with them at a price – the mail-order side of things being even bigger as a consequence. But it's the shop that is the holy of holies, the knock-three-times-and-ask-for-Joe routine giving the impression, perhaps intentionally, more likely not, of a carefully hidden hole-in-the-wall place, like some closely guarded secret that only the dedicated are privy to.

FLOPHOUSE TO THE FAMOUS

The one place that encapsulates the history of Chelsea, New York, and the way its character has changed over the years, is also its most famous establishment: the Chelsea Hotel, or Hotel Chelsea as it's officially called.

From an apartment building in the 19th-century theatrical hub of 23rd Street, to boho flophouse during and after the Depression, to arty address in the '60s and '70s, to its current trendy status complete with a fashionable club in the basement, the Chelsea has a story rivalled by no other hotel in the City, not even such celebrated lodging places as the Algonquin or Waldorf-Astoria.

'A building, 12-story brick, with brownstone trimmings, flat for 40 families, 175 x 86, mansard, brick, and new patent roof, cost $300,000; owner George M Smith,' was how 222 West 23rd Street was described in the *Real Estate Record And Guide* of 20 January 1883, when it was an experimental co-operative apartment building,

New York's first. It was also for its first ten years or so the City's tallest building, before the era of the skyscraper was launched with the Flatiron Building.

At the time, 23rd Street, albeit briefly as it would turn out, was the main thoroughfare of New York theaterland, much like the Bowery before it and Broadway subsequently. But as the focus of theatrical development shifted up to midtown locations around 40th Street and Broadway, so real estate developers moved into the area, changing the financial climate for property generally – and for the Chelsea apartment co-op in particular, which went bankrupt.

That was in 1905, after which the building became a hotel, and quickly became a favoured residence, either temporary or permanent, of writers, artists and other members of the creative bohemia. Early notables staying there included Mark Twain and the actress Sarah Bernhardt (who allegedly brought her own sheets and quilt); in 1912 it housed the survivors from the *Titanic*; and in the 1920s and '30s it was home to often-feuding groups of Stalinist, Trotskyist and other left-wing activists.

It was home to hard-drinking writers from across the Atlantic, Brendan Behan and Dylan Thomas, in the 1950s, as well as the new breed of beat generation authors and poets, William Burroughs and Gregory Corso among them. It provided a roof for Arthur C Clarke in the 1960s – he wrote his classic *2001: A Space Odyssey* there in its first form as a short story entitled *The Sentinel*.

Also in the '60s, it was where you would find various luminaries of the pop art movement – Jim Dine, Claes Oldenburg and Larry Rivers among them – and most significantly the Andy Warhol crowd. Several of his so-called 'superstars' from his mixed-media Factory, including Viva, Ultra Violet and Edie Sedgwick, lived at the Chelsea, and he used the hotel as a location in his 1966 movie *The Chelsea Girls*.

The hotel has been celebrated in various other ways as well. Leonard Cohen stayed there and wrote 'Chelsea Hotel No 2' as a result. Likewise singer Joni Mitchell wrote her 'Chelsea Morning' while she was a guest. There have been a long line of rock stars on the hotel register, including Bob Dylan – who wrote the epic 'Sad Eyed Lady Of The Lowlands' while living there – Janis Joplin, Patti Smith, and, of course,

Sid Vicious and Nancy Spungen, the former stabbing the latter to death in the hotel's most notorious episode.

Ex-Ramone Dee Dee wrote on the hotel's own website: 'I've lived at the hotel on and off since 1974. I wrote the songs for Ramones, I get my best work done here at the hotel because it's quiet; the walls are really thick. I just want privacy. The hotel is a nuthouse, but this is the place where I feel the safest. No matter where I go, the Chelsea has always been a home for me. I tried to live a suburban lifestyle, but couldn't handle it because of all the traveling, commuting.

'I like the hotel because it's a very social place. I saw a suicide here: a woman jumped from the ninth floor, and I heard a big noise when she hit a cab and landed right in front of me. The woman lay there for four hours, covered by a tarp, before they took her away. But out of this terrible thing, quite a few friendships developed as people in the building rallied together.'

Now the place boasts Serena in the basement, a plush cocktail lounge with low black velvet couches and pink pillows, which attracts a smooth, vaguely trendy but not particularly boho crowd. They are certainly not as interesting as the residents upstairs, who manage to maintain the Chelsea Hotel's fine tradition of eccentricity – and outrageousness from time to time – as befits a residence of such pedigree.

RADIO, RADIO

I once had a very complicated conversation with a friend in Memphis, Tennessee, which began with my referring to a certain kind of fan or obsessive enthusiast as an anorak. My friend, a Memphian born and bred, was unfamiliar with the word, even in its correct usage regarding an item of waterproof clothing. This led me to explain that the slang use came about because the anorak was a favoured apparel of trainspotters, at which point he interjected, 'And what's a trainspotter?'

I was then obliged to launch into an account of what trainspotters were; until then it had never occurred to me that they might be an exclusively British phenomenon. My description that followed must have sounded like the famous Bob Newhart monologue of 'Crazy Walt' Raleigh introducing tobacco from the New World, my colleague incredulous as

I explained that in the UK grown men can be seen waiting on railway platforms for hours, in all weathers, to take down the numbers of railway engines they've not 'spotted' before. Why? I had no idea.

I was reminded of all this when standing in a queue – sorry, 'on line' – awaiting the doors to open for the biannual WFMU Record Fair, 9:30am on a Saturday morning on Chelsea's West 18th Street. It was a boiling hot day, so there wasn't an anorak (or American equivalent of) in sight, of the clothing variety anyway. But there were scores, and the line was growing by the minute, of the US version of the anorak-as-fan. Geek? Nerd? They must have a word for it. Dress-wise, they could be called Heavy Metal T-Shirts; there were certainly a lot of those in evidence.

Two guys behind me were talking energetically about some old 45s on the Roulette label one of them had found. Now I'm as big a fan as anyone of vintage rock 'n' roll, but these T-shirts were getting excited about the *serial numbers* rather than the music. Similarly, in front of me another character was showing his pal a battered-looking album sleeve, which presumably he was bringing to sell or get a valuation on, claiming that this was the rare *laminated* version, of which only a few were ever produced. Wow!

By the time the glass doors of the Metropolitan Pavilion were swung open at 10am sharp, the line of eager punters had grown to several hundred strong. And, within sight at least, all of them seemed to be men, something else the T-shirts had in common with the anoraks.

As the fans trooped in, paying their $5 (£3) admission at the door, the music inside was already pounding out as dealers and vendors set themselves ready, prepared for the onslaught. Rows of trestle tables lined with cardboard boxes and plastic crates, each filled to capacity with vinyl LPs, CDs and 7" vinyl singles, ran the length and breadth of the hall. T-shirted dedication notwithstanding, any music fan couldn't fail to be sucked in by the sheer quantity of material there to browse through. And unlike even the most comprehensive record store, there's an added element of finding the unexpected at such events, coming across some much sought-after treasure or forgotten musical memory purely by chance. It's a lottery, and all you have to gamble with is your time.

We've all been anoraks in our own way of course, we all have our 'best of' lists mentality regarding some niche or genre, redolent of Nick Hornby's hero in *High Fidelity*. To shelve alphabetically, by genre or date: that is the question for vinyl, and now CD, addicts the world over. All of us get absolutely fanatical, usually almost secretly, about something or other.

My particular passion has been The Shangri-Las. From the seagull simulation intro breaking into the heavy chords, like waves crashing on a dark shore, when 'Remember (Walking In The Sand)' first hit the UK charts back in 1964, I was hooked.

I was always a bit of a snob when it came to The Shangri-Las. 'Remember' seemed far 'purer' than the eventually more famous and much-parodied 'Leader Of The Pack', and as I got deeper into the detail of their record catalogue I found myself concurring with Pete Townshend's expressed view that the totally traumatic 'Past, Present And Future' was simply one of the greatest pop records ever to be made.

By this time it was becoming an obsession. Even though The Shangri-Las only made 30-odd tracks, mostly singles, I was on a mission. As well as first-release copies on the original Red Bird label – licensed in Britain by Pye, as fellow SL freaks will recall – I grabbed weird re-releases at record fairs just like the New York shindig. I've even got a version of 'Remember' put out on a cheapo-cheapo label that turned out to be a pre-mix without the essential seagulls.

Of course, this kind of completism can never be fully satisfied, even with artists as limited in their output as The Shangri-Las. Pity the Dylan collector (I've only got 40-odd albums on vinyl and CD), or Beatles buff, where out-takes and bootlegs outnumber the vast amount of official stuff ten to one.

At fairs like this, if you're prepared to dig around for another hour, another day even over the weekend, you're bound to come across your own golden chalice. Depending on your music – it might be R&B, jazz, doo-wop, punk, techno or classic pop – the ark of the covenant could be in the next pile you've just got to thumb through.

But I didn't have all day, unfortunately. I was here specifically to talk to one of the organisers. Not about the record fair as such – record fairs are record fairs all over the world, through this one was certainly bigger than most – but the organisation behind it. It was the twice-yearly fundraising event for one of the most adventurous and ground-breaking independent radio stations in the country: WFMU, based in New Jersey.

WFMU has been a pioneer of what has come to be known as 'freeform' radio, still an unusually open-minded take on the medium even in North America, where most none-commercial radio stations cater for a specific specialist taste, be it punk rock or classical music, current affairs or religion. Even those who do 'mix it' to a degree certainly don't follow an electronic jazz session with a karaoke phone-in, or invite listeners to contribute 'found-sound' tapes, or broadcast a morning show promising to play 'The finest in Micronesian doo-wop, Appalachian mambo, Turkish mariachi, pygmy yodeling of Baltimore, Portuguese juju, Cajun gamelan, tuba choirs from Mozambique, Inuit marching bands, Filipino free jazz, Egyptian Kabuki theater and throat singers of the Lower East Side.'

I sought out Brian Turner, the station's music and orogramme director, on the WFMU stand near the entrance to the hall. He was keen to stress from the start the open-ended approach that makes it pretty well unique in broadcasting.

'WFMU is a listener-sponsored freeform radio station that exists on its own, broadcasting out of Jersey City. We have an internet broadcast as well, we cover all of New York City as well as the Catskills, plus New Jersey, eastern Pennsylvania, the Hudson Valley. The station has been a pretty eminent proponent of the freeform philosophy, which is we play all types of music and non-music: we have everything from experimental music shows to experimental talk shows, anti-phonograph programmes, country, talkback shows, found-sound tapes. And we play straight-ahead pop and rock, as well as world music, strange music from the past and present, people's home recordings, they all fit into a big, open format that our DJs adhere to, and that's what we generally stick to and what we look for in our DJs. The people that do radio for us aren't students or professionals, but rather just people out there with a little interest or philosophy, and they all kind of group together in this big giant mishmash of disparate personalities programming music.'

The description 'freeform' came from a so-called 'free forum' style of radio pioneered by a Seattle station, KRAB, in the early 1960s; it was first introduced on WFMU by a DJ Vin Scelsa, and it was a trend with a number of FM stations for a while. It soon went the way of many trends-for-the-sake-of-it however, and even WFMU dropped the approach for a while, until adopting it more vigorously than ever in the mid '70s.

Until the mid 1990s the station had been based in Upsala College, an independent university that eventually went bankrupt. That was the trigger for it to go it alone, relying not on any kind of sponsorship but purely listener-funded support.

'We don't do any ads at all, not even underwriting. We exist on listener contributions. Once a year we do an annual fundraiser where we go on the air and ask for pledges for two weeks in exchange for our T-shirts and prizes, things like that. And then events like this record fair, which we have twice a year, are also fundraising for the station, and once in a while we'll do the odd benefit concert where we have bands like Stereo Lab, Sonic Youth, ESG, these kind of bands will play on behalf of the station and we'll raise money that way. But the station's completely listener supported.'

Broadcasting from Jersey City after the split from its host college, the station now has a string of transmitters giving it considerable coverage.

'We have a few transmitters, we have one upstate and one in the New Jersey area. We used to be part of a college, a university college in East Orange which is where the station was located, but that college went out of business in 1994 and we bought the station, and in 1998 we moved the station off the campus, which was abandoned, to our own home base in Jersey City. We have our own studios in Jersey City now, which is where we operate.'

The non-music shows, Turner feels, are an essential element in the complexion of its output, and the way it connects with what he refers to as the 'creative community' centred in New York.

'We have some talk shows, we have some call-in shows, but they're not the usual type of "morning dew" type thing you hear on commercial stations. We tend to involve the listenership a lot more, and address topics that don't get addressed much on radio. A lot of artists and creative types in the area usually listen to our station, so we'll have a lot of guests that fall into their interests. But we also have fun: we have a programme called Seven Second Delay where very often listeners will be routed to go and do things in the course of the hour and we'll hear back. So it's kind of fun and unusual like that.

'We also have a few lecture shows every year, we hold various lectures, like Buddhist lectures, we have a show called Joe Frank, which is kind of a floating, surreal drama that's pre-recorded by this guy in California that involves strange stories... We also have a show where found tapes are played of people singing in the shower, that sort of thing.

'But we're very involved with the creative community, the music community in New York. A lot of people here today are DJ-ing, and over the weekend, famous personalities in underground music, they help the station out by coming in, and we do a lot of live music performances on the air with various artists coming to town, whether it's garage, rock or klezmer [rock and jazz heavily influenced by traditional Jewish music], you know, all kinds of stuff.'

A while back, WFMU put out a fundraising brochure, which ran a blurb that gave some insight into the ongoing philosophy of the station.

'When WFMU's signal inhabits your radio, you're giving that device more power than an appliance should reasonably be allowed to have. At its best, WFMU makes you ransack your own home in search of a blank cassette on which to capture the magic of our programming. Or your radio might pull you across the room like a magnet because you can't turn it off fast enough, so horrid is the discharge spilling out of our meager little transmitter. Then there are the times when your crystal set compels you to increase the volume because the music we're playing needs to be heard L-O-U-D. Or s-o-f-t, as you clench your teeth and wait out a somewhat irritating phase of programming that wouldn't be so painful if it would-simply-move-on-to-something-else. Soon. A radio tuned to WFMU has these abilities because good radio requires good listeners who are active participants in the programming. WFMU's survival is a testament to the quality of listeners we've been able to attract. And what's so amazing about WFMU is not that we've survived an eight-year string of potentially deadly crises, but that we've done it without selling out.'

It's a philosophy that's helped produce a mode of broadcasting that's unique. Amongst the eclectic mix of music, where else would you find 'Phone Jams' where listeners call up and contribute music through the phone and all the calls get mixed together like they were playing together in a band, or live broadcasts from the parking lot outside the transmitter shack when the studio lost electricity (it was a polka trio that played live in the rain). Or the audio artist who did a composition for two radio stations involving WFMU and WKCR. Or 'Radio War' with WKCR, which involved teams of programmers hurling sound effects at one another which was broadcast on both stations. The list of ground-breaking broadcasts goes on and on: some fun, some serious, all challenging.

WFMU now broadcasts on the internet, with listeners as far afield as Australia, New Zealand and eastern Europe, but it's as an essentially 'local', albeit far-ranging radio station that it functions best. Even the station magazine *LCD* (*Lowest Common Denominator*) – the issue I picked up at the fair included articles intriguingly entitled 'Extraterrestrial Communists', 'Bedspring Symphonies' and 'Monsters of Geographical Rock' – is more like a satirical fanzine than a radio programme guide.

As Brian Turner points out, the station enjoys a lot more real independence than most 'community' broadcasters that depend on public subsidy in place of advertising revenue: 'A lot of public radio stations funded by the government in America don't have the freedom to put out what they want, they've gotta lobby for certain causes, in exchange for subsidies. But since our station is completely listener sponsored, we exist on our own...' It struck me that freeform radio could be neatly defined as a truly *free form* of radio, certainly as represented by WFMU's history of pioneering broadcasting.

4 Village Voices

Greenwich Village is one of those places tailor made, by its geography and history, for that curious aspect of tourism known as the Walking Tour.

Geographically, it fits all the criteria. First of all, it's small enough to be walkable, bounded by 14th Street in the north and West Houston in the south, and extending westwards from Broadway to the Hudson River. It's accessible, right there between Chelsea and SoHo, leading to midtown and downtown respectively. And within those borders it's physically interesting, and by and large attractive, with a fair share of greenery, some quaint (ie old) buildings and even a park or two.

And, most significantly, it's where the grid system that serves Manhattan so reliably finally disintegrates into a maze of streets, some still with numbers, most with names, built over the years in the haphazard fashion common to cities the world over before the 20th century.

One of the most confusing aspects of this, which throws native New Yorkers and fledgling taxi drivers as much as strangers, is coming across the junctions where West 4th Street meets West 10th, then 11th and 12th, given that the whole by-number system is based on the streets, like avenues, running parallel.

You need a map to work it out, but it's a doddle for the folks on a Walking Tour; they're all clutching maps anyway so know exactly what's going on.

Historically, the Village is prime territory for the Walking Tour. As well as Architectural Walking Tours, taking in beautiful streets and courtyards of old brownstones, clapboards, and houses that date back as far as the 18th century, there are Literary Walking Tours – often ending up like pub crawls from the Cedar Tavern to Chumley's to the White Horse – and even tours visiting sites of the folk-music revival. As I write this, I've just come across a Bob Dylan Village Walking Tour. No doubt, perhaps held only once or twice a year, there's a Beatnik Walking Tour, even an Abstract Expressionist Walking Tour, and almost certainly a Greenwich Village History Walking Tour.

But assuming you don't require the camaraderie of a dozen like-minded anorak-wearers, listening to the route-by-rote litany of a student-on-vacation-turned-guide, the Village has even more to offer the inquiring traveller who wants to get at least a hint of what made the area synonymous with New York bohemia. And indeed, what still makes it tick today.

THE 'HORSE ON HUDSON

When the great Welsh poet Dylan Thomas downed one last shot of whisky on a November night in 1953, staggered outside the White Horse Tavern and collapsed, the fame – and infamy – of the hostelry at 567 Hudson Street was guaranteed for ever. After falling into a coma at the nearby Chelsea Hotel where he was staying, the bard was rushed to St Vincent's Hospital, where he died.

Today the pub looks much as it always did, although the clientele of after-office locals, students from nearby NYU and inevitable tourists doesn't lend the place the bohemian *frisson* that it exuded in the days following Thomas's death, when it became a magnet for writers, musicians, painters and such through the 1950s and early '60s.

Built in 1880 at the corner of Hudson and 11th Streets on the western edge of the Village, the White Horse is one of the few wood-framed buildings remaining in the city. For decades, its proximity to the warehouses and docks of the Hudson made it a longshoreman's hangout with no literary pretensions to speak of, until the early 1950s when it began to attract visiting Britishers, no doubt reminded of the pubs back home.

A Scottish poet, Ruthven Todd, was said to have introduced Thomas to the place, and soon the Welshman had adopted it as his New York headquarters on his visits to the City, his drinking bouts there becoming the stuff of legend. Even before his final demise, folk would visit the bar just to watch him noisily carouse, and today a plaque – as well as a plethora of portraits and such – commemorates his passing. Although the tavern's never been noted for its food, on the anniversary of his death they even serve the last meal Thomas ate there before he died.

Although Dylan Thomas and his drunken soirées made the 'Horse world famous, it was a watering hole for a number of other noted writers, whose presence also helped establish it as a literary landmark. Norman Mailer, William Styron, James Baldwin, Lawrence Ferlinghetti all hung out there, Anaïs Nin was one of the few women writers who frequented the bar, and staff writers from the pioneering 'alternative' newspaper *Village Voice* came over from their original offices on nearby Sheridan Square.

Jack Kerouac, while living in a house across the street, was a frequent customer, and his heavy drinking resulted in him being forcibly ejected more than once. He even found 'Kerouac go home!' scrawled on the wall of the men's room, an episode later referred to in his book *Desolation Angels*.

It was also a musical hangout, with folk-scene luminaries like Theodore Bikel and Josh White joining in sessions in the back room, usually led by the Irish singers The Clancy Brothers. During his early Village days, Bob Dylan would drop in regularly to hear the Clancys play.

The old wood and glass of the main bar hasn't changed at all over the years (though some extra side rooms have been added) nor items like cottage pie on the modest menu, and although the jukebox seemed a lot, lot louder the last time I was there – it was Friday night and packed to the doors with young drinkers – in the daytime it's much as it always has been, the one concession to some kind of urban chic being the tables that are now out front on the sidewalk during the summer.

BOHEMIANS, BEATS AND BEATNIKS

The history that is evident in a little-changed – one could say deliberately preserved – spot like the White Horse is there for all to see and feel, while other addresses evoke recollections that are far more retrospective, personal even, unacknowledged and unmarked.

There's no fancy plaque outside 161 West 4th Street, located between Jones Street and Sixth Avenue, but this is the building in which Bob Dylan rented his first apartment in New York, with his girlfriend Suze Rotolo. He moved into the two-room flat in December 1961 after checking out of the Hotel Earle at 103 Waverly Place (now refurbished as the Washington Square Hotel, but still relatively inexpensive), where he'd lived briefly after arriving from his native Midwest earlier in '61.

The couple stayed here through 1962 and were famously photographed walking along Jones Street towards West 4th for the cover of his second album *The Freewheelin' Bob Dylan*.

Parallel to Jones Street is Barrow, where the Barrow Street Ale House occupies the same converted 19th-century stables at number 15 that was previously the marvellously named Café Bohemia. In the heyday of bebop in the 1950s, the Bohemia showcased some of the greatest jazz names to walk – and blow – on the planet, including Cannonball Adderley, Miles Davis, John Coltrane and Charles Mingus. Jack Kerouac was a frequent member of the audience, as was the writer Diane de Prima who described seeing Miles Davis there '...slick and smart as they come, exchanging sets with Charlie Mingus, cool then and cool now'.

Sometimes, all that remains are the ghosts.

Ted Joans, who lived just down the street at 4 Barrow, was another Café Bohemia regular. Ted was a central character on the Greenwich Village beat scene, a poet and painter who is one of the unsung heroes of that era. Pick up any photographic account of the beat generation and you'll spot Ted somewhere, his 'bop' beret stereotypical of the black jazz-poet hipster. Indeed, when the whole beat thing started to get overexposed publicity wise, Ted was one of the chancers who would hire himself out to posh suburban house parties as 'Rent-a-Beatnik'!

Joans had his tiny one-room 'pad' on Barrow in the early 1950s, with space for one single bed and little else. Nevertheless, when a neighbour lost his own place, Ted let him move in, along with the neighbour's 'house guest', the great jazz saxophonist Charlie 'Bird' Parker, who was 'between homes' at the time. Joans later described how they would even share the bed: 'Bird said, "I don't come in till three or four in the morning – you cats should get up and let me sleep."' Which they did.

When Parker, among the greatest sax players who ever lived and a founding figure of modern jazz, died in 1955, it was Joans who first instigated the 'Bird Lives!' graffiti that started appearing all over New York City in the wake of his death. Interestingly, Parker is one name whose residence in the East Village, from 1950 to 1954, is marked with a plaque at 151 Avenue B, the section of which outside the building has been renamed Charlie Parker Way.

In the 1960s Ted Joans divided his time between New York, Paris and Timbuktu in the African Republic of Mali, with sojourns elsewhere in between, and it was during one such UK stopover in the late '60s that I first met him. I have fond memories of searching the Edinburgh branch of Woolworth's for a particular size of toy pistol with which to fire Maltesers at the audience during a 'happening' entitled 'Chocolate Astonishment', which he was staging later that day as part of the annual Fringe Festival.

Ted died on 25 April 2003 at the age of 74. He was alone in his apartment in Vancouver, Canada, when he died. His body wasn't found until nearly two weeks later.

The aforementioned *Village Voice* was where the actual ad for the 'Rent-a-Beatnik' service appeared, the inspiration of one of the staff journalists. It appeared in December 1959, and is worth quoting in full: 'Add Zest To Your Tuxedo Park Party...Rent a Beatnik! Completely equipped: Beard, eye shades, old Army jacket, Levi's, frayed shirt, sneakers or sandals (optional). Deductions allowed for no beard, baths, shoes or haircut. Lady Beatniks also available, usual garb: all black (Chaperone required).' A later ad in the paper listed the services rendered as including 'Model for Photographs/Entertain or Read Poetry/Play Bongo Drums'.

But from its very first edition in 1955, the *Voice* performed a far more radical function than that of an eccentric ad sheet. It established itself as the liberal voice for all of the City, not just the Village, and prestigious writers who worked on it in those early days included Frank O'Hara, Norman Mailer and Nat Hentoff. It was also the pioneer of 'listings' magazines, for many years the only comprehensive 'what's on' for New York. It's still here today, of course, and still a voice of reason in often unreasonable times, not to mention the most reliable weekly guide to everything that's happening and more so. Hit the streets without it at your peril.

A LITERARY SPEAKEASY

Predating the White Horse Tavern as a writer's rendezvous, Chumley's is to be found, with some difficulty it has to be said, round the corner from Barrow Street on Bedford. The discreet entrance is without any signage, a small menu is all that tells you what's inside, walk by and you'll miss it. Likewise the 'back door' on Barrow is similarly nondescript, both this 'exit' and the 'entrance' a clue to the bar's colourful past.

In 1922, Leland Stanford Chumley, who'd been a labour organiser, waiter, artist, newspaper cartoonist and editorial writer in an already action-packed life, opened Chumley's as a 'restaurant'. But from the start it also operated as an illegal speakeasy, selling alcohol along with the food. Prohibition had been introduced a couple of years earlier, not to be repealed until 1933. The bar's concealed entrance and handy getaway exit were a response to the constant threat of police raids during those years.

Almost as soon as it had opened, word got out about its 'hidden location', and writers, journalists, playwrights and other intelligentsia found their way there. Illustrious patrons included F Scott Fitzgerald, John Steinbeck, Lillian Hellman, JD Salinger, Eugene O'Neill and Orson Welles. During the 1940s William Burroughs would start an evening with dinner there, and Lawrence Ferlinghetti was another of the earliest beat writers to frequent the place.

Its walls are decorated with first-edition book covers of the writers who drank there, but this is no recently contrived sop to the tourist trade or literary history-seekers, 'twas always so. In 1948 the proto-feminist existentialist writer Simone de Beauvoir wrote in *America Day By Day*, calling it 'The Literary Speakeasy of Greenwich Village': 'The room is square, absolutely simple, with little tables set against the walls, which are decorated with old book jackets. It has that thing rare in America: An Atmosphere!'

The Chumley's tradition is upheld today, with artists such as David Mamet and Woody Allen among its customers, the latter having shot some of his 1999 jazz film *Sweet And Lowdown* on the premises. Like the White Horse, and McSorley's over in the East Village, it's one of those genuine time-warps you come across in New York where things haven't been reconstructed for their nostalgia value, but simply never changed very much. Big-band jazz hits you when you walk in, the house dog gets under your feet, and the range of real ales includes Chumley's own selection from its on-site microbrewery with names such as Golden Goose Lager and Bulldog Bitter.

The big downside of late has been that its reputation for 'atmosphere' has somewhat overtaken it in recent years. These days anyone visiting Chumley's who doesn't want to rub elbow-to-elbow with noisy parties of pub-crawlers, office outings and even sailors when the fleet's in town, would be advised to stroll in during the afternoon or very early evening. Like many places with every good intention of resisting commercially motivated change, it's become something of a victim of its own success at doing just that.

CEDARS ONE AND TWO

Up in the northern reaches of the Village, where University Place leads into Union Square, the Cedar Tavern between 11th and 12th Streets is another establishment that was a catalyst in the days when bar culture was central to the artistic life of the area. Before moving to its present location in the early '60s, it was lower down at number 24 that it was the gathering place of the artists of the New York School, the Abstract Expressionists like Jackson Pollock, Willem de Kooning, Mark Rothko and Franz Kline. Literary names frequenting the old Cedar – it was actually called the Cedar Street Tavern – included the beat triumvirate of Ginsberg, Kerouac and Gregory Corso, and the bar was a far more spartan affair than its successor. There was no TV, no jukebox, just basic tables and stools, which is just as well considering the frequent fights that broke out as passions ran high among the painters and writers.

After making way for the redevelopers and a luxury apartment block, in 1963 the new Cedar opened at 82, and was still a magnet for the creative milieu through that decade, regulars including Tuli Kupferberg, leader of the folk-rock-punk pioneers The Fugs, and the musician/composer David Amram. According to Bob Spitz's *Dylan: A Biography*, DA Pennebaker, Dylan and Bobby Neuwirth met to plan the shooting of *Don't Look Back* in the Cedar Tavern.

Since then nothing's changed as far as the decor's concerned, the lines of booths at first almost indiscernible in the dark gloom, which persists whatever time of day it is. The newly draconian no-smoking regime in New York's bars may make the outlook a little clearer as you enter the Cedar, but not much.

THIRTY YEARS OF MIXIN' IT

To a greater degree than in most 'bohemian' quarters around the world, in Paris, London or wherever, the artistic lifeblood in Greenwich Village has been driven by music and musicians as well as by painters, writers and others. And today, as always, the venues and entrepreneurs that promote that music are a part of the creative fabric as much as the musicians themselves, who, in the main, aren't able to afford to actually live in the Village anymore.

One such long-standing promoter is Allan Pepper, who has been running the Bottom Line club with his partner Stanley Snadowsky since it first opened nearly 30 years ago. I call in the club during the afternoon, before the early-evening opening time. The band's doing a sound check, roadies are busying themselves, bar staff are getting things ready: the usual buzz of fully lit activity before the lights go down for show time.

The act on stage is Soozie Tyrell and her band, second billing to singer-guitarist John Hammond. New York singer and instrumentalist Tyrell is a time-served session player best known recently for playing violin with Bruce Springsteen, but with an impressive list of other credentials spanning 25 years – including Sheryl Crow, Carole King, Hammond himself and Springsteen old buddy Southside Johnny – which culminated in her debut album *White Lines* featuring members of Bob Dylan's backing outfit. Since the album's release she's received long-overdue rave notices (including one from yesterday's New York *Daily News*). And listening to her just running through half a number, then into another for the sound guys, everything they say is true.

Allan Pepper appears and introduces himself. We've spoken briefly on the phone and he leads me backstage where we can talk. The band's still playing as I switch on my recorder and begin the interview; listening to Tyrell and looking at the week's line-up of attractions, it seems a pretty mixed bunch. Has it always been that way?

'Let me just say this…the one thing that we tried to do from 1974 till now is to be consistent. We had a decision to make when we opened, and the decision was what kind of a place did we want it to be. Did we want it to be a rock room, did we want it to be a jazz room, a folk room? And we decided that what we want is a music room. Because we thought specific audiences become too fickle, so as long as you were presenting names they knew, whether it was in any genre – folk, jazz, rock – they'd flock to you, especially if it were a well-known artist. But if you couldn't do that, and if you had to present lesser-known names, it would be a little more difficult to maintain the flow.

'That was number one. Number two, because our taste was eclectic, it seemed much more of an interesting challenge to put together a music room with a thread or the through-line of continuity being quality. So we made the commitment to present the best of any given genre, based, I guess, on our taste and our perception of what was available at any given time. And we also made a commitment to vary things as much and as well as we could, to make it interesting for us. As far as I'm concerned, as far as this room is concerned, nothing has changed from the standpoint of what we present. We present the best of what is available to us in any given genre.'

Some things have changed of course. The business for one, and the pure function of running a business: 'The business has changed enormously. When you think about it, when we opened this place, people were buying vinyl, now they're buying CDs; a CD was a thing that wasn't yet heard of at that particular time. And there were no fax machines and there was no e-mail.'

Likewise, the world outside, and that part of the Village in particular at 4th Street and Mercer – on the New York University campus – has seen huge social and economic changes over three decades.

'Not everybody you knew was running out and getting sushi at any given time…there was no barrage of Mexican restaurants all over the place, there were no Korean grocers on every corner. And, where we located, this area was virtually – after six o'clock at night – a deserted area. There were only manufacturing and office buildings around, so people went home; there was no nightlife. Now, if you walk one block over to Broadway there are all kinds of stores including Tower Records, Barnes & Noble Bookshop, Borders Bookshop, McDonald's, all kinds of clothing stores and stuff like that, and the action on that thoroughfare – well, there's a lot of people there, including till 11, 12 o'clock at night, there's a lot of traffic.

'I was told, I don't know if this is true or not, that one of the reasons Tower Records decided to open down the block was because we were here, so it meant that obviously there was a population in this area – not to mention that we are on the campus of NYU.'

The Bottom Line actually celebrates its 30th anniversary in February 2004. Throughout that time it seems to have carved a niche for itself, presenting solid names from the broad field of rock, folk and jazz (with the emphasis on the first two) in a more 'regularised' environment than the often chaotic informality of most rock clubs.

The 400-seater club is often described as a cabaret venue because it presents separate performances each night – sometimes one, sometimes two – and this has evolved over the course of the years to attract a more mainstream audience than that catered for by specialist jazz, rock or folk venues.

'When we opened, the shows originally on the weekends were 9pm and 12am and during the week 8:30pm and 11:30pm, and now – I guess in terms of the City as such and what nightlife has become – we have changed our hours. Now this isn't brand new, this is at least 12 to 15 years ago, we changed our hours to 7:30pm and 10:30pm to accommodate more people on the second show being able to get out a little earlier – you know, for work the next day.'

Despite this slightly streamlined programming more usually associated with the 'corporate' environment of a genuine cabaret, the Bottom Line has retained what Pepper describes as the 'Mom and Pop Candy Store' operation of a hands-on ownership.

'This place has been owned for 30 years by two people, myself and Stanley Snadowsky. I am here or he is – well he's not now 'cos he's living in Vegas – but I am here every single day. So this is not an absentee ownership; we are not owned by a corporation with deep pockets. You are having a problem with something during the course of the evening, if you're a customer here, you can actually make a complaint to the boss. You can't say that in many other places. Many places are large places, they are controlled by major corporations, they have a booker who books the show, in many cases he's not even there, or if he is there he's not there for every single show. So this is a "Mom and Pop Candy Store". And if we're still successful that is possibly one of the reasons.'

But the main reason for the club's success still seems to be the broad-based booking policy, one that attracts tourists as much as locals, but discerning tourists all the same. A booking list – scanned at random – that headlines names such as Nancy Griffith, Bruce Cockburn, Robben Ford, David Lindley, Marshall Crenshaw and Loudon Wainwright III can hardly be called bland. The trick that Pepper and Snadowsky have honed over the years has been to identify acts that balance quality kudos with commercial – and often international – appeal.

'We have a mixture of everything. And I think on any given night the percentage of our population differs. If it's during the summer and there are a lot of Europeans who come here, and we have a particular jazz act or a particular act that might mean more in their country than it does here, we'll do a lot of tourists. There's also a Bottom Line in Japan, in Nagoya, so there are a lot of people who come here 'cos they're curious to see what this place is like.'

A current topic is the newly legislated smoking ban across the City, extending to bars and restaurants as well as other indoor venues. It's a huge bone of contention among promoters and such that I talk to, though Pepper doesn't see it like that, the club having imposed its own curb on smoking over a decade ago. Wasn't that an unusual measure for a music club?

'Well, it was, but I have to tell you something. First of all, neither my partner nor I smoke, and if you were in a room night after night with people smoking, you're really exposed to it. And for other patrons who don't smoke it's problematic.

'And there's something that nobody thinks about. For the artist who's sitting on stage who doesn't smoke, with people right under them, blowing up, they are inhaling as they're singing all the smoke into their lungs. It's not healthy for the artist. So the musicians, they're inhaling this, even if they don't smoke.

'And so it really wasn't fair to people, but we allow people to smoke in the sense that they can go outside and have a smoke and come right back in. But now you can't smoke in any place in this City.'

Pepper concludes with a story involving a Beatle, English tourists and a New York superstar nobody had heard of a year previously.

'Three weeks ago we did a show on a Saturday night and we had a surprise guest who we knew was gonna appear, which was Ringo Starr. Ringo Starr came in and played with his band, The All Starrs. But we couldn't advertise this to the public as it was a special…but the word got out and the show was sold out.

'A couple came up to the box office, and they asked for tickets. And my person said, "I'm sorry, we're sold out."

'They didn't seem to be too upset about it, they were clearly tourists. And they said, "Okay can you tell us where there's a good pub or…"

'And I realised very quickly they were English and I could not let them walk away without having this opportunity. So I found them two seats and I said, "I'm one of the owners, I'd like you to come in, pay for your tickets, I'm gonna get you seats. And I'm not going to tell you why: we have a special guest, I'm not gonna tell you who it is. But at the end of the evening, when the show is over you're gonna be flabbergasted that you came from London to here tonight to see who this artist is."

'So they said okay, they were very nice, they took it in the spirit and they trusted me, they put down their $40 [£25] – 'cos it was $20 [£12] a ticket – they had no idea… This was a show we do on a regular basis called Required Listening, it's four acts, which we feel our audience should know about. And it's our way of turning people onto music that they might not be aware of. And it's a very classic evening, it's a little different.

'They came in for the second act, which they liked a lot, and at the intermission I couldn't wait to tell them who it was [following] so I ran over and said, "Listen…"

'When I told them Ringo Starr, their mouths dropped open and they said, "You're kidding me."

'And I said, "No, it's really Ringo," and they wouldn't believe it. I said, "Here's a little hint, look at the stage, see that bass drum that has the word 'Ringo' on it? That might be a clue!"

'But I think the thing that thrilled them the most was that in the encore Norah Jones came out and sang. She sang "A Little Help From My Friends" with Ringo. So these tourists, this man and wife, came from London, unbeknownst to them, to see Ringo Starr, Norah Jones and four other acts that they had never heard of.

'That was a nice New York City moment.'

A GOOD TRIP, A GREAT RIDE

Back in the very early '60s there was a very film noir-style TV cop series set in New York called *The Naked City*, with a voice-over narrator ending each 30-minute episode with the mantra – 'There are eight million stories in *The Naked City*. This has been one of them.' – which became something of a catch phrase at the time.

After meeting Paul Colby, proprietor of the Bitter End club and music-business veteran extraordinaire, I mused to myself that there were probably eight million stories worth retelling in his head and I'd just heard a few of them.

It was like emerging from a cinema in broad daylight having watched a particularly inspiring film, as I hit a sunny lunchtime Bleecker Street, my mind reeling with the thought of how much the man I'd been talking to had touched upon the whole gamut of American popular music, in a career spanning nearly 60 years.

I spoke to him initially on the phone from my hotel room: he was at home in New Jersey and he explained he wouldn't be in the City, at the club, for a couple of days, by which time I would be leaving for London. When I suggested a telephone interview when I got back to England, he'd have none of it. 'If you can get to the club tomorrow, I'll be there at 11am, we've gotta do this properly.'

I was there a little bit early, outside the club with its familiar blue awning and wooden façade that's been a landmark since 1961, between La Guardia Place and Thompson on Bleecker Street. Paul, however, was there already, buzzing me in as soon as I pressed the bell on the side doorway, which leads straight up an untidy stairway to his office. He greeted me with a big smile, sitting slightly hunched over a chaotic-looking desk, a baseball cap on his head, with thin arms gesturing me to sit down.

Paul Colby is a remarkable 85 years old, and still running the Bitter End as he has done since 1967, but his story goes way back before that to the 1940s when – after briefly studying the saxophone but choosing art school instead of music, then doing army service during World War II – he was to brush shoulders with legends-to-be like Benny Goodman, Duke Ellington and Frank Sinatra. He began at the beginning.

'My background is very unusual. I started in 1945 working for Warner Brothers Publishing – music publishers – then I went to work for Benny Goodman's company Regent Music Publishing with (his brother) Harry Goodman, and met a lot of celebrities and became friends with some of them.'

Colby's role in the publishing business was as a song plugger, getting live artists to use songs, and hopefully record them or perform them over the air.

'Some of these friendships lasted for years, like Duke Ellington, I was very close to him, 'cos I did a favour for him and we became good friends...Tony Bennett I still see, and I used to work for Frank Sinatra.'

This was during the period when Sinatra had already been a big name as a band vocalist, with hit records to his credit, but had hit a downturn before he became the superstar that he did in the 1950s in both movies and music.

'He had a publishing company called Barton Music. And as a plugger there I used to do publishing work, and then somehow or other, he hung around the office every now and then, I started doing favours for him, and all of a sudden 50 per cent of my time was with Sinatra, doing chores for him, hanging out with him at the Hampshire house. He would call the office and tell me to come on over and hang out; this was before he became a star again.

'So it was pretty lonely days for him; he was ostracised from a lot of people because this was when he left Nancy, his first wife – a lot of people didn't like him for that – so it took a while. Then, when he got the movie

From Here To Eternity, everything changed, and his talent overcame his adversities, and he became a star again.

'I tried for years to get in touch with him, but it wasn't easy, he was protected by too many people. But for a short period of time, around 1950, we were very close, I was with him almost all the time. I even took his girlfriend Ava Gardner to the ballet. I did a lot of little things like that for favours…he couldn't do it, I filled in…and I picked up people from the airport for him, bought presents for him, and he was great to me, I loved him.'

A move out to California for a smaller publisher didn't work out. 'I got lost in the wilderness out there, it was overbearing, like a cliquish town, I did all right but I didn't do well, I was fired…'

Deciding to work his way back to New York, as a stepping stone Paul took an all-girl band on the road as road manager.

'It was supposedly four or five girls, a jazz band, travelling through the south, and then back to LA. And it was two white girls and two black girls, and the two white girls we had to make up every night! We were found out in New Orleans and we were run outta town!'

Paul recalls the incident, back in the days when 'Colored Only' and 'Whites Only' signs everywhere were the norm in the deep South.

'We stopped at a gas station and the guy – I had a Lincoln Zephyr, a 1942 Lincoln, it was a huge car – and a white guy driving four black girls…well, a state trooper pulled me over for going 18 miles [29km] an hour in a 15 mile [24km] zone! We stopped at a gas station and filled up with gas, and were told to "Get out, now!." That was 1949 when segregation was pretty heavy.

'In one bar in Harrisburg, Mississippi, I was standing in the audience and there was a cop next to me, or a deputy, and he's looking at the girls very closely… I was thinking, "Holy shit…I hope he doesn't find out, spot the white girls."

'Anyway he says, "Blah, blah, blah," and I don't know what the hell he's saying.

'So a black guy in the audience, standing next to me at the show, says to me, "Did you ever hear of segregation?" That is not what I *heard*, but that's what the cop had *said*, because his accent was so heavy. So then he says to me, "He's got two notches in his belt."

'I said, "Jesus, let's get outta here" – which we did. It was scary times, at the time.'

By the time they got to Oklahoma City, Paul decided to call it a day and head, as planned, for New York, where he took up making furniture, a hobby he'd developed in California, which now became the unlikely – and long-term – route back into the music business.

'Someone found out I was very handy, they knew about my craft as a furniture maker. It was somebody at Decca Records, she asked me to make something for her – I wouldn't say design – and soon I found myself suddenly in the furniture business. I made furniture for celebrities – Miles Davis, Dianne Carroll, Tony Bennett, Cy Coleman who was one of my first customers, and a lot of other people in the business.'

His reputation spread as he was recommended by one star name after another for his contemporary designs, his work even getting featured in magazines like *House Beautiful* and *House & Garden*. He opened a showroom and expanded – or, as it turned out, over-expanded.

'I got a lot of publicity, I did well – but I over-expanded. There was a recession – I started to get too big for my britches, and I had six workers, which was great, then I got to 13 workers, and…I couldn't control it anymore. So I had to give that up. I didn't go into bankruptcy but I gave it up.'

The furniture business lasted through the 1950s and early '60s, and when he finally gave it up Colby decided it was time to return to the world of music, albeit a world that had changed radically since he'd last been actively involved in it.

A friend by the name of Billy Fields, who worked for Fred Weintraub, the owner of the Bitter End, told Paul they were looking for a manager for the club. The folk-music world of Greenwich Village hadn't ever been his scene, and initially he turned the offer down, seeing his future back in publishing, not running a 'coffee-house nightclub' in the Village. But he reconsidered, thinking it was at least a stepping stone back into 'the business'.

'So here I was in 1967, not knowing what I was doing; I'm uptown with Tony Bennett, Dianne Carroll, all the publishers up here. Then all of a sudden I'm down in the Village with Tom Paxton and Tim Hardin and Simon and Garfunkel, Phil Ochs, and these are all strangers to me 'cos I was not into folk music. At one point I thought Simon and Garfunkel was a drugstore, I really did...'

The Bitter End, of course, had been a pillar of this scene since it opened in 1961, and featured all the great names of the early '60s folk 'revival' that was to evolve into folk-rock – an area equally alien to Colby. But the club seemed to be on the way down, or rather the way out. By 1967 rock *per se* had taken over as the music of a new 'alternative' youth culture, so the Bitter End with its mainstay of established folk acts was almost as out of touch as Colby felt; as a consequence, it was on the verge of bankruptcy. Turning it round was a challenge Paul Colby couldn't resist.

'When I finally got here I floundered for about a year. They had certain acts that played here, like I mentioned Tom Paxton and some staple names that we had. But then I had to go find my own, because the owner Fred Weintraub had bought the film rights to the Woodstock Festival, and the record deal, so he became a big mover, as they say, in Warner Brothers. He became vice president of the Creative Department, and I was here trying to figure out what the hell to do.'

Crucially, Colby booked Joni Mitchell, who was just starting to happen, and, during her well-attended appearance there, The Everly Brothers' manager came into the club to listen.

'He sat down and looked around, and he was amazed. With his Armani suit and his Rolls-Royce parked outside, this was a whole new world, a hippie world, if you wanna call it that. And she [Mitchell] was going very well. I said, "Look, put the Everly Brothers in here, they haven't done well for a long time, they're doing all right but they're only playing lounges, no rooms."

'" I was thinking about this for a long time..."

'"Okay, here's your chance." I put in the Everly Brothers and we sold out.

'In those days we had two shows during the week and three shows at the weekends. So that's 14 shows a week; all the acts played 14 shows. So I mention names like Jackson Browne, Bette Midler, they all played 14 shows. That was the norm of the day, all the coffee houses played the same amount of shows. And we sold out every show.'

Colby was getting his teeth into booking now, and broadening the mix of acts as he developed a revived Bitter End fit for the late '60s and the decades to come.

'I started to get the hang of booking. I booked Ricky Nelson, and I even decided – 'cos everything was changing, the folk era was not over, but diminishing – in order to survive I can either stay a folk club like all the other clubs and die, or go on and become a cabaret, or a nightclub or whatever you wanna call it. So I started to book Stan Getz, Stevie Wonder, Larry Coryell, Chick Corea, offbeat acts, country acts, Johnny Paycheck, I even booked Willie Nelson but they cancelled, I booked Kris Kristofferson, Mickey Newbury, I went all over…but my pull at the time was to book the acts that the audience will like, in good taste. I didn't have to like them. For instance, Chick Corea, I like him, but I'm not gonna buy his albums and take 'em home. I'll buy Gordon Lightfoot but I'm not gonna buy Chick Corea. But you couldn't get in the door for Chick Corea.'

In 1974 Colby became the owner, completing the transformation of one of the legendary coffee houses from the hootenanny days of the early '60s to one of America's leading nightclub venues, but very much a new style of nightclub.

'Then I did Bette Midler and Lily Tomlin, I did offbeat things, and we became a nightclub. So at the time, before MTV, when the record companies needed me, this was the premium nightclub in New York. As a matter of fact the Bitter End is the last surviving nightclub of its kind in America. It started as a coffee house, 41 years ago. All the other clubs have closed. There were hundreds of clubs of this type, the Café Wha?, Max's Kansas City, the Café a Go-Go, in Chicago there was the Quiet Night, the Boarding House in San Francisco, the Salvador in Washington DC, there was one in Florida… So they were all over.

'When a record company sent an artist out on tour, they did the circuit. It doesn't exist anymore. Now MTV changed everything. One shot, there you are, you're a star. In those days you had to leave an artist in a nightclub to build himself, get the press and promotion, and get to disc jockeys…'

He waxes philosophical for a moment, contemplating a future that will continue while he's able to make it do so.

'So what we do now is play a lot of acts that we think are up and coming. Record companies still come here looking for the new ones, 'cos we think we have the prime of the new acts. And that's what we do, and we do it very well. We're not getting rich, but we're paying our bills, we're surviving. You can't put your money away, but at least you're paying the damn bills and staying alive. And I guess it's just thinking ahead, and being young in spirit and feeling at the heartbeat.'

Paul's office desk, and any other handy surface nearby, is heaped with the usual stuff of the music business – CDs, promotional photographs, flyers – and mountains of memorabilia, from dog-eared photographs to signed pictures to news clippings, around the walls. And posters, dozens of posters chronicling the great bills that have been presented at the Bitter End over the years. Legendary names many of them, and many of them Paul is pleased to call friends, a theme he returns to while mentioning the autobiography that was published in 2002, *The Bitter End: Hanging Out At America's Nightclub*.

'I have made some very good friends – if you notice my book, you see the preface, it says "Foreword by Kris Kristofferson". We're still friends to this day – I like to think we've made friends.

'As a matter of fact I saw that play across the street about the Mamas and Papas. We haven't seen each other for years, but the Mamas and Papas played here, and we're still friends. We're doing a concert in Washington Square Park on 26 May together; I'm gonna try and get Peter Yarrow [of Peter, Paul and Mary] and the cast of the Mamas and Papas.'

The concert is to be a fundraiser for the Greenwich Village Folk Music Museum, which is still at the drawing-board stage, of which Paul is a trustee. Active support has come via events like this, and a CD, from a host of names associated with the old – and more recent – Village folk scene. The list is impressive, including Pete Seeger, John Hammond, Odetta, Judy Collins and the one-time leader of the NY folk-rockers The Lovin' Spoonful, John Sebastian.

'We have some property we're looking at right now, we have to come up with finance – we have a fundraiser. We're talking to developers, a new area right down here; they've cleared two blocks and there's a new complex coming in. They're building it in stages so…they need to know how much space we need because the city requires subspace...we wanna put a restaurant, a school, a museum, do a whole thing, so that's my next project.'

The CD – which is a live recording of a benefit concert for the museum project held in June 2000 – is on Bitter End Records, the label Paul started to help launch up and coming artists. This enthusiasm for new talent, and his involvement in the museum, is reciprocal help for that which he received from that same musical community when the club was threatened with closure back in the early 1990s, and Peter, Paul and Mary, Kris Kristofferson, George Carlin and others staged a benefit to help keep the club open.

At one stage, Paul also opened a restaurant next door. Called the Other End, it was popular with Village folk and others who just wanted to hang out sometimes, not necessarily come to the club to hear a particular act. One such regular as soon as the place opened its doors in 1975 was Bob Dylan, who'd begun spending a lot of time in New York again, frequenting places like the Bitter End he'd first known when he hit Manhattan as a young hopeful a decade and a half earlier.

In fact, it was at the Other End that the whole plot that resulted in the now-legendary Rolling Thunder Review was hatched, the all-star touring outfit that Dylan famously took on the road at the end of '75. The extravaganza included, at various times, Joan Baez and ex-Byrd Roger McGuinn, poet Allen Ginsberg, Dylan's old friend vocalist/guitarist Bobby Neuwirth, guitarist Mick Ronson, Village folkie Ramblin' Jack Elliott, violinist Scarlett Rivera, vocalist Ronee Blakely and many others.

'It was a typical night when Bob Dylan comes in, hangs out in the club and then goes next door. Bobby Neuwirth was here, who was also a good friend, Bobby hung out here a lot. This night they come into the restaurant, they're sitting at a table and they start taking their guitars out. And they're sitting at a table in the corner, and Bobby Neuwirth came over to me and said, "Bob and I are talking about doing a tour. No name yet, we wanna do a tour – can you handle it?"

'I said, "Of course" – although I had no idea at all. I was thinking, just get people who've done this before for the organisation, that's all it takes. I said, "Let me give you my idea. My thought is not to do 20,000 seaters, let's do 5,000."

They said, "That's what we have in mind."

'I said, "Great," and one thing led to another.'

The tour line-up – which Dylan wanted to have the ad-hoc feeling of an old-time travelling medicine show – evolved equally casually, often there in the Other End.

'One night Jack Elliott's [appearing] in the room. "Jack, get over here, you wanna do a tour?" Jack's drunk, he says okay, he thought it was two guys who were drunk, 'cos when I mentioned it a couple of weeks later, he had no idea they meant it. So then who walks over? Ronee Blakely – she was in the room, so she was on the tour.

'Another time in walks Roger McGuinn. I said, "Roger, come over here" – he was on the tour. Anybody who was in the room was on the tour.'

Colby helped set the tour up with backing from the agent William Morris, but record-company politics and such saw him quit after it got under way, but not before he'd gone on the road with it for some of the first memorable dates. The idea was to forewarn a small venue like a college campus hall just a week or so before, via handbills and word-of-mouth, that the 'circus' was coming to town. There was much speculation as to how the name evolved, but Dylan claims it came to him when he heard thunder rolling out from east to west as he sat outside his house one night, only to be later pleased to discover that in Native American lore the expression 'rolling thunder' means 'speaking truth'.

Paul points to an old photograph pinned to the wall, of windswept men walking on an otherwise deserted beach. It's him and Dylan, the night of the opening gig at Plymouth, Massachusetts.

'They stayed at a place called the Sea Crest Motel, about 20 miles [30km] away from the site in Plymouth, Mass. It was about a 5,000 seater [in fact records set it at even smaller, only 1,800]...the town didn't believe it, Bob Dylan coming in.'

He shows me another picture 'of Bob and me sharing a sandwich at the hotel after the show. But do I know Bob Dylan? No. I have a theory about Dylan. You know Dylan but you don't know Dylan. Nobody knows the real Dylan.'

One incident, recounted in Robert Shelton's biography of Dylan, no doubt endeared the singer to Colby. The latter threw wine in the face of one of his customers who he'd caught making a bootleg tape of a Dylan show and kicked him out, so Dylan could play the Bitter End with no hassles.

Colby tells me of the time he visited Dylan in his townhouse just a couple of blocks away on MacDougal Street. It was actually two houses – 92 and 94 – converted into one, which Dylan and his wife Sara moved into in 1969.

'Kris Kristofferson was here. Kris said, "Let's go visit Bob Dylan."

'I said, "Well I don't really know him that well…"

'So we went to visit Bob Dylan, knocking at the door. His wife comes by and she says, "Who's calling?" and opens the door a little bit.

'"It's Paul Colby and Kris Kristofferson." She went and five minutes later the door opens, we go inside. Now let me tell you something – I pictured this was an *English* setting, they were having tea! It was all so *proper*, no one was playing guitar, there was no music, we just talked. And then, thank you, goodnight, and we left. I used to go with Kris a lot, we used to visit all these guys, they used to play guitars and hang out and just get a little stoned…but this was nice. He had two houses, with a big yard. That was in the days when that guy used to steal his garbage…'

He's talking about the notorious Dylan fanatic AJ Weberman, who would go though the singer's trash cans on MacDougal to literally pick over any personal detail he could glean from the rubbish. Colby once described him as, 'Revolting even to look at…if you saw him on the subway you'd change seats.'

As Colby stresses, Dylan is 'difficult' to get to know, but Miles Davis's reputation in the antisocial stakes was legendary, though Paul was unaware of this when he struck up a friendship with the trumpet giant.

'I was close to Miles Davis. Someone said, "You're the only white guy he ever liked!" Whatever, I was a friend of Miles Davis's for quite a while. I went to the Apollo Theater with a friend of mine, also in the music business. Backstage [Miles] grabs me and throws me outta there in a playful manner, and starts to wrestle with me. And when we leave, this guy, Duke Niles was his name, said, "I don't believe I saw that."

'I said, "What are you talking about?"

'He said, "He's got the biggest chip on his shoulder." Well, I didn't know about it, but I found out later.

'It was when he got beat up by the cops in front of Birdland...'

He's referring to the incident in 1959 when Davis was savagely beaten by two policemen while taking a breather outside the club where he was playing, the charges against him of assault and disorderly conduct subsequently being dropped.

'So the next night or whatever, I said, "Gee Miles, I'm sorry, what happened to ya?"

'He looked at me and said, "Where the fuck were you when I needed you?"'

As I leave Paul Colby I promise to pass on his regards to Roger McGough when I get back to England. He remembers the poet fondly, and pulls out an old signed picture to show me, from when McGough was part of the Liverpool 'satire' trio The Scaffold, appearing at the club in 1969.

Another memory from a life rich with memories.

'I've had a good trip, I've met some wonderful people. I met Lady Day [Billie Holiday], I had dinner with George Burns, Louis Armstrong was a good friend. My life has been full, for me it's been a great ride...'

And with every memory, a story. Eight million at least.

5 South Of Houston, Below Canal

New York loves its acronyms such as PATH for the Port Authority Trans Hudson, CUNY and SUNY for City University of New York and State University of New York respectively, and MoMA by which the Museum of Modern Art is universally known, but for the visitor the most important to understand are those relating to districts.

The most familiar of these are SoHo, which stands for the area *South of Houston* Street, and TriBeCa, referring to the *Triangle Below Canal* Street. Less-used abbreviations of this kind include the easily understood NoHo, which is gaining in popularity, and the trendier (like the neighbourhood itself) NoLiTa, which is the area between Lafayette Street and the Bowery, just *North of Little Italy*.

My favourite, which has mainly local usage but enjoyed a faddish currency in the 1970s, is DUMBO, for the area Down Under the Manhattan Bridge Overpass.

SoHo is in many ways a southern extension of the West Village, replete with boutiques, restaurants, bars, small art galleries and budget clothes outlets, stretching down the west side of Broadway (to the east of which lies the Lower East Side), after which one finds oneself in TriBeCa.

For the first-time visitor to SoHo there's no better way of getting a good feel for the district than by spending an hour or so in Fanelli's Café. Established in 1872, it's a regular no-frills bar with friendly staff. Pictures of boxing heroes line the walls, with the bar itself running down one side of a long room and tables for diners down the other. There's a room at the back where you can also eat: the food is basic pub fare, hamburgers and such. But the place is first and foremost there for drinkers, who sit or stand the length of the bar. It's a genuine neighbourhood watering hole, with a core of local regulars, plus a lot of passing trade.

When I was there last, it was the day before the total ban on smoking in bars and clubs kicked in. Below notices announcing the approaching deadline, regulars puffed madly on cigarettes as if it was their last. Presumably the perpetrators of this new prohibition hoped that in many cases it was. Ashtrays were full, the air blue. If this had been in London, we'd say these folks were smoking for England.

Fanelli's is on the corner of Prince and Mercer Streets, and just a block away from Broadway. This downtown section of Broadway bears little resemblance to the neon-lit Great White Way of midtown theaterland, the home of the Broadway musical. Down here, cut-price clothing warehouses and street vendors selling bootleg computer software compete for space with the small galleries, bookshops and restaurants.

Heading down Broadway to where it edges on Chinatown at Canal Street, a right along Leonard Street brings us into TriBeCa and an institution that's even marked on some maps – the Knitting Factory.

SOUNDS FROM THE FACTORY

Originally on Houston Street, the Knitting Factory has long been associated with avant-garde jazz, but that label has always belied the choice of music available to customers on any given night. Located in a vast old warehouse-type building, its various rooms offer what manager Shay Visha calls an 'experience' unrivalled in other rock and jazz places in Manhattan: the opportunity to wander from space to space 'pick 'n' mixing' performances in the same evening.

The evolution of the club has been in many ways unique, developing as it has from a specialised club catering for a recognised minority taste to one of the major venues on the Manhattan scene. It's a history that dates back to 1987, when it was started by Michael Dorf and his partner Louis Spitzer, initially as a means to financing an independent record label. Like so many club ventures, the prospect of building up a venue from nothing was daunting in the extreme, as Dorf explains on the club website.

'We had found an old, dilapidated Avon Products office on Houston Street between the Bowery and Broadway. The rent was $1,800 [£1,100] per month for 2,000 sq ft [185 sq m] on one floor in a four-story walkup. The place was really a mess: yellow painted plaster chipping off the walls, a rotted wood toilet, and piles of Avon products scattered all over the floor. When we were trying to come up with a name, our friends suggested calling it the Dump. The initial idea was to have an art gallery/performance space that sold coffee, teas, and a small assortment of foods... But my real motivation at the time was to earn enough money to live and to cover the rent for Flaming Pie Records.'

The story goes back to Madison, Wisconsin, when Dorf started Flaming Pie Records 'out of necessity' after getting involved with a band called Swamp Thing. The band were led by Dorf's old friend, guitarist Bob Appel, who asked Dorf to manage them. The name of the club came directly out of this, when Swamp Thing tentatively decided to call their second album *Mr Blutstein's Knitting Factory* after the sweater factory in Wisconsin where Appel had worked a few years earlier.

By the time of this second LP, although the band had played New York dates in places like CBGB and the Peppermint Lounge, they were still based in Wisconsin. Dorf, however, had moved to Manhattan. Wheeling and dealing on behalf of the band, and the fledgling record label, which was run from his new apartment on East 10th Street, Dorf came up with the idea of the music venue to subsidise his business.

The initial policy when they opened in February 1987, after months of rewiring and general renovation, was to open as an art gallery and coffee lounge in the daytime, and an open-ended 'performance' venue in the evenings, with poetry readings, mixed media, jazz and so on. Whatever, almost inevitably the first live band to play there was Swamp Thing, with a meagre audience made up of friends from Madison.

As with many such ventures, the timing – though unwittingly – was just right. The jazz scene was polarised between the 'established' styles represented in venues like the Blue Note and Village Vanguard and the new generation of free-jazzers, funk-jazz players and such whose only 'public' space was their own self-generated loft scene. The latter, by and large, had no commercial places to play. Likewise with rock. Apart from well-established venues like CBGB – where straightforward punk bands were literally queueing to get a spot – there were hardly any places presenting the more experimental new names.

When Dorf ventured into having Thursday-night jazz sessions, the first thing that he did was advertise in the *Village Voice* for a jazz outfit for the residency. He wasn't really aware of who was who on the current scene, but felt that the 'Jack Kerouac smoky jazz-club' was the kind of atmosphere that he wanted to create. So when keyboard player Wayne Horovitz replied to the ad, and subsequently offered to take care of finding other bands as well as his own quartet, Dorf was more than satisfied.

Via Horovitz's connections in the freeform jazz world, the influx of cutting-edge names began to create a buzz around the Knitting Factory from there on in. An early attraction was avant-garde saxophonist John Zorn who was working on a project involving two guitars backing a poetry reading in Korean when introduced to Dorf. The latter premiered the piece as a midnight show, and there was standing room only for the first time in the club. It wouldn't be long before names like Horovitz, Zorn, guitarist Bill Frisell and British bass player Fred Frith made the Knitting Factory synonymous with avant-garde jazz worldwide.

Dorf's next move in establishing the venue's ambience involved Raymond Ross, a jazz photographer of long standing who happened to live in an apartment above the club. His black-and-white pictures went back to the 1950s, intimate shots of some of the greats of the music world including Miles Davis, Count Basie and other names, and Dorf set up a month-long exhibition of his work on the walls of the venue. To publicise it – and the club generally – he produced posters featuring some of the shots, announcing that the musicians on them were currently appearing at the Knitting Factory, which of course they were!

Dorf fly-posted them all over downtown, occasionally getting phone calls asking what time Louis Armstrong – or some other long-deceased legend – was playing.

The Flaming Pie record label meanwhile was struggling along, with albums by Swamp Thing and a couple of other Madison bands making no profit on the balance sheets. Radio stations and customers at the club would ask for recordings of the avant-garde jazz as the club was fast gaining a reputation. Rather than Swamp Thing's latest LP, Dorf realised that the next step was to start making live recordings there in the club.

What resulted initially was a *Live At The Knitting Factory* radio series of eight one-hour shows including John Zorn, Bill Frisell, Fred Frith, Arto Lindsay, Steve Coleman and many others. This side of things began to take off as more and more stations aired the shows, and even though some of the club attendances were literally in single figures, Dorf felt that the recordings on those same nights were possibly history in the making. But what catapulted the recording side into the major league was when Dorf met up with the head of A&R at the giant A&M Records.

Through 1989 and 1990 A&M released Volumes 1 to 4 of *Live At The Knitting Factory*, recorded in an in-house studio set up with the aid of the record company's advance on a four-year contract. Things turned sour, however, when A&M was bought by the multinational Polygram for $500 million (£320 million) and the modestly selling Knitting Factory material had no future in the balance books of the corporate giant. Eventually, when its contract expired, the club managed to regain control of the entire back catalogue of recordings.

By this time the Knitting Factory was becoming – potentially at least – something of a brand name, and the next step was to take it on the road. The first event outside the confines of the club walls was a festival staged in New York as an alternative to the annual JVC festival, the 'establishment' event run by George Wein as a successor to his Newport Jazz Festival of the 1950s and '60s. The project didn't make much money, but it garnered huge publicity, so much so that it attracted the attention of a Dutch arts centre, which booked a 'Knitting Factory Festival' package of over 30 musicians.

News travels fast on the musicians' grapevine, and by the time the package got back to New York it was the talk of the (musical) town. So much so that George Wein accepted Dorf's proposal of a series of 'Knitting Factory Goes Uptown' concerts to complement his JVC Festival, in the Alice Tully Hall in the Lincoln Center, right next door to the prestigious Avery Fischer Hall where the big names like Dizzy Gillespie and Ella Fitzgerald were playing.

More European tours followed, where both the musicians and Dorf recognised there is more of a following for avant-garde jazz than in the United States, but the club remained the core of the Knitting Factory enterprise. In 1991 the touring Knitting Factory finally took on America – the northwest corner at least – with a three-band trek that covered cities from San Francisco up to Vancouver in Canada. The European trips had taught them a lot about on-the-road merchandising and so on, selling T-shirts and CDs to help cover costs. The tour also produced the first CD release – *Knitting Factory Goes To The Northwest* – on their label, Knitting Factory Works, their first such venture independently since Flaming Pie Records.

The main feature that distinguishes the club today, its variety of rooms with simultaneous performances taking place, had its origin in the late 1980s in the previous premises on Houston Street. John Zorn asked if he could stage a series of five rehearsal-concerts with his new band Naked City at the club, but as the acts for the week in question were already booked, Dorf negotiated a deal with the antiques shop next door to present the shows at the 'Knitting Factory Annex'.

At the 11th hour, with ads in the press and posters all over New York, the shop pulled out of the deal, leaving the club – and Zorn – well and truly in it.

What happened next was fortuitous to say the least. For years, since they'd opened in fact, the club had been getting grief from Estella, proprietor of Estella's Peruvian Restaurant, which was right below them on the ground floor of the building: complaints about the noise and such. They offered to hire the space for the five nights of Zorn's shows, but ended up buying out her lease. When Naked City debuted, it was in the new expanded Knitting Factory, which would be made permanent with a new connecting staircase, plus a small performance space called the Knot Room where Estella's kitchen used to be, for poetry readings and acoustic sets. Suddenly the Knitting Factory was a three-room venue, as it's remained ever since.

The move down to Leonard Street in TriBeCa came in the mid 1990s. It's a bigger venue, and its expansion has been accompanied by a broader brief as far as booking policy is concerned, away from a jazz-centred to a wider-based programme, but still concentrating on interesting creative music that you might not hear elsewhere.

Shay Visha began working in the club as night manager in November 2000. I met him between his supervising drink deliveries, checking on bar-staff rotas and the usual daytime preparation that goes before opening a night-time venue.

'I started off as a night manager: the night manager's job is basically to arrive on site at around 3pm in the afternoon, and then take control of everything that's happening, during the course of the evening. That's from organising the bartenders who come in, setting up the bar inventories, making sure the bands are loaded in, making sure the staff turn up on time, know what they're doing, making sure the bands are happy and the deals are all clear and all that, making sure they are set up properly, paying the bands at the end of the evening, settling up, reconciling all the bars, and then being the last person out – basically, closing up. Normally the bar is open till 2am or 4am, so you can either be outta here by 4am when the bar closes at 2am, or 7am when it closes at 4am.'

His background, as with so many on the management and entrepreneurial side of the music business, is as a working musician, not in the US, but the English Midland city of Leicester. A British Asian, he was born in Kenya, his parents migrating to London in 1966, where they lived for four years before moving to Leicester.

It was in Leicester he began playing keyboards – 'not very well!' he hastens to add – before forming a band called Defector III with four other local guys when he was 15 years old.

'We toured around Europe, spent a lot of time touring around Europe and all that kind of stuff. We were four Indian guys from Leicester, we did pop punk, you know, we all grew up with that 1976 punk explosion, so that's what we were motivated by – The Jam, The Clash, Costello, all that... And then we split up, and I went out of the whole music scene for around five years.'

He finally ended up in New York in 1995 after running a booking agency, United Sounds, for some time, which still functions today from its base in Switzerland.

'Me and my partner started a booking agency in Europe, and he's now in Switzerland and we still have that booking agency. We bring a whole bunch of American bands over and do the whole European tour thing. It's based in Lausanne, it was in Zurich, but we've just moved back two weeks ago, to Lausanne. And there's a big annual music festival in Zurich – well we started that. So yeah, he's doing really well over there.'

The agency business started just around the time the post-punk ska thing was breaking in England, a phenomenon led by bands on the 2-Tone label also emanating from the Midlands, in Coventry. Curiously, this was what led to Visha's move to the States.

'Because we were taking a whole lotta bands on the road, we kinda got caught up in this whole ska revival that went on with The Specials, the 2-Tone thing...so we started taking a lot of those bands on the road. And there's a band called Skatalites – you know them? Well, they're in their 60s and 70s now. And they invented the whole ska and rock steady and reggae thing...so we brought them to Europe and they wanted us to become their managers. So one of us had to move over here 'cos they were based in New York. So that was the reason I moved over here.'

Coincidentally, when the Knitting Factory moved to its TriBeCa location, the first band to appear on the first day in the Main Space was the Skatalites, booked in by Shay long before he ever worked at the club.

'It was kind of bizarre that I ended up working here. For the first five years I've done like seven or eight shows here, with the Skatalites. So I know the club from that perspective, and I know a lot of other clubs all around the city, and around America as well. I've spent more time on the road than I did actually in New York. Every time I came back to New York I would never go out, 'cos you'd just spent five weeks on the road, you know, partying every evening. I moved up to my home for four weeks, just to get back to some sort of normality, and then get back on the road again.

'So I didn't really know a lot of New York, except for the clubs that I actually played in. And the guy who was second-in-charge here (his name was Ed Greer – he's no longer with the company) had been trying to get me to work here for about four years, so I finally caved in and said, "Okay, I wanna have a bit more of a normal life, I don't want to live out of suitcases from a hotel room. Yeah, I'll take on the night manager's job."'

With Michael Dorf's recent departure, Shay's role changed accordingly, in the way that often happens in company shuffle-politics.

'I used to work three days a week up until the beginning of this year [2003]; the club went through a bit of a transformation recently where the previous owner Michael Dorf is no longer part of the company. A guy called Jerry Hoffman is now in charge of the club and the Knitting Factory label...that took place six or seven months ago.'

All this impacted on the Knitting Factory's other club, which is located out in LA.

'It's only been around for about two years. It's definitely more LA-ish, with a VIP room, and everyone gets treated like a superstar there. Anyway, our previous general manager here, she decided to quit and move onto other avenues that she wanted to pursue. So they hired a new general manager, Scott Long. But then, while this changeover was taking place, Scott got moved up: his title now is director of national clubs, so he's basically in charge of both the Los Angeles and the New York clubs. And that gave me the opportunity of moving into the kind of general manager role here, you know, 'cos it gives me the comfort of having Scott around, and if I go away on tour again there's always somebody here, and vice versa when he's in LA, I can do more of the stuff that he would...it's a good little partnership that works out. So that's the basic story of how I got here.'

The last few years, Shay's few years involved with the club, have seen its booking policy broaden considerably.

'It started off with more the poetry and avant-garde jazz thing, but as time and finances dictate, you start having to broaden your outlook, but that's where it's got its branding name from. I think I've been there for two and a half years, but the fact that this [new location of the] club opened eight years ago with a ska band tells you something. So that [the avant-garde tag] was like a good way of getting known for the club, but it was never what it did all the time. The club always booked a wide variety of acts, from cabaret to burlesque shows to poetry reading, to soloists, to hip-hop shows, to hardcore, to punk, to whatever. I think the way we like to describe our booking policy is interesting, live music that's cutting edge. You can walk into this space on any given day, and we will have a minimum of seven bands playing.'

The arrangement of rooms and spaces has in some ways evolved over the years, rather than being planned from the start; the current management, and that means Shay Visha, feel it's time for some major refurbishment to take place.

'We go through a lot of little minor changes and some major changes, you know we're remaking a lot of the spaces, and are resoundproofing a lot of the rooms. This particular floor, we're knocking out that wall, making it a bigger space; it needs a little bit of a facelift, the club. I mean it's been kinda like *maintained* over the last eight years, a dab of paint here and there, nothing major.'

Like all clubs – especially apparent with the lights on, as we sit in the Tap Bar as a barman readies for the evening's business – the decor gets frayed around the edges, things get to look tired after a time. Like the man said, time for a bit of a facelift.

'This first year of the restructure of the club is basically gonna be devoted to redefining a lot of the spaces, and just really thinking about the stuff that's been kinda added on over the last eight years, adding a live webroom and such, just rethinking things like that so that it's fresh for the people, but still has a lot of its old character.'

But basically they'll be keeping the current arrangement of the Main Space where the headliners appear, the Old Office Lounge, which only has a one-drink minimum cover for most shows, and the Tap Bar, which also features live bands. There's also the Alterknit Theater, which was undergoing the first of the impending renovations when I was there.

'The best thing about this place is the actual space. It's so cool, you have the Main Space – and that's what it is. Then you go one floor down and come to the Tap Bar: we have 18 beers on tap, which is more than most regular bars have. We keep our prices as if they are bars, we don't wanna charge venue prices, we always have free music. So, for instance, if you were a paying customer you could actually walk into this bar right now without paying a cover, you could sit at the bar all evening, there'd be live music being played, different bands every evening, our cheapest beer is $3 [£2], the most expensive beer is $5 [£3], pub prices, bar prices, you know.'

Shay's enthusiasm borders on the evangelical – it's clearly inspired by more than just 'doing the job' – but it comes over as great PR for the club as well. And there's nothing wrong with that.

'So it's an interesting location, the way the club is actually arranged, it's not like any other experience people have. If you go to somewhere like the Irving [Plaza] or the Bowery [Ballroom], you're going there specifically for the act playing that evening. Here you can be completely surprised.'

The sheer ecleticism of the programming has been an education for Visha as much as anyone.

'It's weird – I had such a great knowledge of the whole ska scene because I spent a lot of time in that genre. Then within three months of working here…I mean my scope of music is still not as wide as I'd like it to be, but it has definitely expanded, like incredibly. When people told me who John Zorn was I had no idea. Most people would know, but not me 'cos I was so into the whole ska thing…'

Presumably the broad spectrum of music means a similarly diverse customer base?

'We get a great amount of visitors, the club is internationally known; we have a lot of Japanese tourists that come in, we have a lot of French tourists and so on. But because of the design of the club, its three floors and three music venues and stuff, what will happen is that because the lower two floors are primarily booked with local acts, we'll get a whole bunch of New Yorkers that will come in here 'cos they're supporting the local bands. Yet at the same time you could have a national tour and a main headliner upstairs that will bring in a whole area of people. I mean people come to New York from Connecticut, Jersey, Long Island, Philadelphia even: it's an hour and a half drive, which in America is nothing, it's just the same as a trip down the road in England. So people will come up for just one show if it's one of their favourite acts.

'Our clientele goes from the 72-year-old guy who's into his favourite style of jazz to 12-year-olds who are into John Mayer. We did a fan-based show here the other day, completely sold out obviously 'cos the place is too small for John Mayer. And yeah, there were 12-year-old kids here who were having a great time!

'A lot of it has to do with our booking; on Sundays we have churches here, in the mornings, there's a whole bunch of kids who come here for that. Then we do matinée shows for kids, so the parents can drop 'em off, do a couple of hours worth of shopping, come back, pick the kids up and go on their way.'

Nevertheless, there are obviously parameters to this open-ended approach. The club draws the line, not so much at a style of music *per se*, but where a genre with a particularly demonstrative following draws a crowd who tend to dominate the general vibe of the club.

'Depending on the kind of show that we have in the space, if it's punk then yes, we'll have a whole load of punks in the area. If it's a hip-hop show, we'll have a hip-hop crowd in here. The hip-hop we're trying to cut down on a little bit. It's not really what we want to be doing a lot of: it's a very awkward crowd. And also hardcore bands. So we're trying to cut down on those a little bit, but we'll have hip-hop shows if it's something interesting or cool, not just done for effect.'

I bring up the subject of the current bone of contention of most bar owners and club proprietors at the moment: the newly imposed smoking ban.

'They started it at midnight on 30 March [2003], and then they decided that they would give bars and restaurants one-month grace period, so that takes effect tonight, basically. So midnight tonight is when fines will start being given out. I'm a non-smoker, but it just seems bizarre coming from England and having that pub culture... I think it's the most retarded thing, just retarded. I can see the reasoning, and they put it to you because of the health thing for your employees, but there's not one bartender or one person who works in a bar or whatever that doesn't go into that knowing that, "Oh, this is not gonna be clean air".

'They're trying to do this in New York 'cos it worked well in LA. But there is one subtle difference between LA and New York, and that's the weather. It works in LA because all year round you can have people standing outside smoking, it's not a problem. Here in November and December, it's −3 or −4°C (25 or 27°F), it's gonna be freezing out there.'

But concerns over what he sees as unnecessary – and often unreasonable – restrictions imposed by the powers-that-be, or just plain circumstance, go far further than just the immediate effects of the prohibition on smoking. They're concerns shared by many other venues in a similar position.

'This club has been here for eight years, and in that eight years the area has changed: it's become more residential in the sense that our neighbours are extremely rich neighbours because the apartments they built around here are multi-million dollar apartments. To afford to live in this area, you have to have a pretty penny. That having been said, they [the new residents] also have a lot of pull because they are rich people.

'So now the community boards are becoming stronger. What happens with community boards is they start ousting out businesses, businesses that have been here before *they* moved in. And so we have to bend over backwards right now to make sure that everything we do, not only in the club, but outside the club, up the block from the club, is OK. We are basically having to police this whole block now, from Broadway to Church. Not only on our side but across the road.

'So what do we do? We have to increase our costs, which makes it harder for us to make a living. We have to hire more people to walk outside to check it's clean and and proper and tidy. When the clientele leaves the establishment we are told to employ staff that will gently guide people calmly off the block, and make them understand that, you know, they had a good time in here this evening, it's in their best interests to move off the block or do whatever. You're harassing your customers, you're telling them to please be quiet, please move off the rail, therefore making the whole experience of coming to the club painful, so what's gonna happen is they're not gonna come. And what happens then? We go out of business.

'And this goes back to the whole smoking ban. You have 7 or 10, 15, 20 smokers outside all the time. But smokers being smokers, they'll go stand outside and have a chat. So here you are again, you're abiding by one rule by moving everybody outside of the club, but then you're gonna get bombarded by all these complaints because now you have 15, 20 people standing outside talking all the time. It's a no-win situation.'

A gloomy picture, which Shay hopes they can in some respect compensate for by good old-fashioned customer relations.

'What we do is in the club we try to make it as comfortable as possible, and then some. We go overboard trying to make the customer feel welcome, welcome them with open arms, ensure that our managers and bartenders are the nicest people that we could have hired, the sound people are the best we can employ, the artists are treated with kid gloves, as if they're the best people on this earth, so that when they come back into the city they go, "Oh, let's go back and play at the Knitting Factory 'cos we had a good experience there."'

He sees these current pressures as the main cause of clubs and bars closing down, and the general shift outwards from Manhattan.

'In the last three years three big clubs have closed down, like Wetlands, which had a great music scene, they closed down; Tramps, which was also awesome. These were venues of this calibre, this size, same kind of people, same kind of bands... Coney Island High was another and they closed down.

'And that's why you see a lot of venues starting up in Brooklyn, Southpaw, Warsaw, NorthSix, that's why that's happening. We want all the fans to get into the city, and then the mayor puts up the tolls on Brooklyn and Manhattan bridges to come into the city, it's gotta be even harder. It's baffling 'cos the city makes so much revenue from bars and tax and stuff like this, they're cutting off a major vein of income for them, and nobody seems to be shouting about it...'

Shay pauses, realising he may be painting an even gloomier picture than intended. He is, after all, talking about a club refurb, live music won't disappear from the City, whatever...

'But you really can't beat the live scene. And the thing about New York is that it is the most influential music market in the world. Everybody wants to come here, everybody's looking for a space to play, everyone who comes to visit wants somewhere to go. The thing for me, the best thing about this club is, you can walk in here every single day, you got free music and there's always something exciting going on in the club, always something weird and exciting that you're never gonna see anywhere else in the City. And that's the beauty of working here.'

CLUBLAND NIGHTS

On the northern border of SoHo, West Houston Street, stand two clubs that, in their own way, represent just a microcosm of the huge Latin-music constituency that you'll find right across New York.

The Zinc Bar at the corner of La Guardia Place is, strictly speaking, a jazz club, but one that features a strong bias towards Brazilian sounds. Although its roster of artists reads like a who's who of contemporary jazz names – Roy Hargrove, Grant Green, Max Roach being among the big names who have appeared there – the eclectic mix of samba, Afro-funk, flamenco and straight-ahead jazz give an exotic feel to the place that *Guitar Magazine* has described as 'New York City's most happening jazz club'. Brazilian and Brazilian-inspired acts from Paul Meyers to the marvellously named Brazilian Groove Ensemble dominate the schedules of the club, the steep steps to which nevertheless welcome committed night-owls of most musical persuasions.

Further along Houston, where it meets Varick Street on the west side of SoHo, stands SOB's, an established part of the world music scene, which it helped launch back in the 1980s. Opened in June 1982 by Larry Gold, the club's mission from the start was 'exposing the musical wealth and heritage of the Afro-Latino Diaspora to as many people as possible', and with this in mind came the name, which stands for Sounds Of Brazil.

At that time, SoHo hadn't become the trendy enclave it is today. Gold's vision paid off, however, and what was previously a mundane family diner on a nondescript corner was transformed into one of the hippest nightspots in the city. Just as the world-music boom was taking off, SOB's pioneered in the presentation of African, Asian, Caribbean and Latin artists to the new trendy crowd who were starting to revitalise the area and change it from its former status as a virtual no-man's-land to one of the City's cutting-edge districts.

For anyone who wants to experience the feel of Latin music in its many forms without venturing to enclaves such as the *barrio* of Spanish Harlem, the programme of SOB's is as good as you'll get anywhere.

From the 'La Tropica' party every Monday, which starts with an after-work Latin dance class, followed by an all-out Latin dance party, through Friday's 'SOUL CITY' new-talent spot followed by a 'Late

Night French Caribbean Dance Party', to the long-running 'Samba Saturdays' featuring Brazilian dancers as well as some of Brazil's most popular live bands, here is the genuine article. Plus some great Latin items on the food and cocktail menu.

Over on Greenwich Street near the Hudson River, where it crosses Spring Street, Don Hill's has been a fixture on many band's gig lists since it was opened in 1993 by – you guessed it – Don Hill. The dive-bar looking corner joint is part live venue, part dance club, with a glam-oriented punky feel that in many ways echoes the trashy New York scene of the early punk era, when the Dolls and Debbie Harry's pre-Blondie Stillettos set the tone. Drag DJ Steve Blush's Wednesday night 'Rock Candy' nights and the once-a-month 'Bitch' nights featuring all-female rock bands, are typical. Even the red booths are reminiscent of the Max's Kansas City of old.

Although jazz is not at the cutting edge of what's new and fashionable in the way it was in the 1940s and '50s, the heyday of still-functioning clubs like Birdland, the Blue Note and the Village Vanguard, it still seems to be part of the fabric of New York. If not in actual live performance venues, it proliferates in many shops and bars as the *de rigeur* background music, and even mainstream record stores have jazz sections rivalled only by those found in Tokyo or Paris. And in a broader sense, New York is synonymous with jazz of one kind or another. There seems a general affection for the music that goes far beyond the earnest fanmanship of the record-collecting enthusiast.

The Jazz Gallery is a SoHo institution that takes jazz seriously, describing itself as a 'cultural center providing exhibition and performance space for work in the arts – visual, literary and musical – that takes jazz as its central influence'. Founded in 1995, the gallery's expressed goal is to present an expanded understanding of jazz as a cultural tradition, which brings music together with other arts, and thus extends far beyond its musical form.

Located on Hudson Street, the second-floor venue features art exhibitions, talks and such, alongside live performance, right in the heart of what it describes as 'the world's greatest concentration of internationally prominent jazz clubs'. The gallery is a not-for-profit organisation chartered as a New York State museum, with events funded in part by a grant from the New York State Council on the Arts. Its gift shop specialises in jazz books, photographs and concert tickets.

The amazing acoustics in the cramped venue have to be heard to be believed, achieving that 'intimate' atmosphere that marks out clubs rather than concert venues as the preferred choice of both jazz audiences and musicians. Current names who feature in the gallery regularly include guitar player David Gilmour and saxophonist Marcus Strickland, while luminaries such as trumpet star Roy Hargrove regularly drop in to jam. It has also featured the legendary bass player Henry Grimes, who after a prolific career with the likes of Gerry Mulligan, Chet Baker and Anita O'Day, disappeared from the music scene in the late 1960s, only to be rediscovered in autumn 2002, after some jazz histories had even written him off as dead!

Further – much further – to the avant-garde end of things, Roulette occupies a space in the heart of TriBeCa, a couple of blocks away from the Knitting Factory on West Broadway. The highly experimental events there, run by trombone player Jim Staley, represent the outer fringe of freeform music, as they have done now for over a decade. Roulette's commitment to 'innovative' music is unswerving, and the place has its dedicated following for what is unquestionably 'difficult' music for most listeners. It also hosts events in other venues: a 'Mixology' Festival in a SoHo venue, the Performing Garage, in summer 2003, included duo tape performances, video-and-movement, a soundtrack and slide show happening, and a presentation billed as 'video-sonic bellydance'.

Both TriBeCa and SoHo represent the process of gentrification that has taken place in lower Manhattan over the last 20 years. SoHo was originally a totally industrial area known as Hell's Hundred Acres, and by the 1960s seemed doomed to destruction by the urban developers. The masses of cast-iron warehouses were saved, however, largely by the artists who'd moved into them for both residence and studio space.

It wasn't long before businesses followed, making the area New York's prime downtown shopping destination.

TriBeCa underwent a similar metamorphosis more recently, with even larger – and now grander – warehouses being converted into living spaces. Here (as Shay Visha was keen to point out) it has been the rich

– and often famous – calling the shots, in the once down-at-heel industrial wasteland. Here the shops are glitzier than in SoHo, the restaurant menus fancier, the property pricier. Given the general dynamics of the housing market, and the area's proximity to the financial district in the southern tip of the island, it comes as no big surprise.

6 Diners, Dinners And Delis

An essential to waking up in New York is experiencing the New York breakfast. This can vary from the bagels and cream cheese beloved of mid-morning shopping ladies in the basement of Bloomingdales to the myriad variations on the Great American Breakfast best found in diners across the city.

The classic diner, a close relative of the roadside diner familiar from a thousand movies and MTV videos, is harder to find now than in years gone by. As for all small businesses in the City, ground rents have soared, but more significantly the eat-on-the-run culture represented by take-away delis and serve-yourself coffee shops has become more and more the norm.

New Yorkers have always eaten, at least snacked, 'on the hoof'. Picture postcards and tourist guides celebrate its hot-dog stands and pretzel stalls. But a sit-down breakfast on the way to work was a part of NY life until relatively recently, now, sadly, largely given way to a swift salad wrap and disposable cardboard cup of coffee. Luckily, supported by casual 'visitor' trade as much as the local workforce, a few good diners still survive.

In what my wife (rightfully, as it turned out) insisted was a totally pointless search for the classic New York diner, I once dragged her – we were staying in midtown at the time – to the now-disappeared Jones Diner at the corner of Great Jones Street and Lafayette, on the edge of the East Village. The red-brick, single-storey building was of the standard diner dimensions: long and narrow, like a railway carriage. (As any diner aficionado will confirm, many classic American diners were actually fashioned from disused railroad cars.) For years it provided cheap, easy eats for cab drivers, people operating the nearby car wash and such. In reality, it was what in the UK we would call a greasy spoon.

With its plastic flowers and ketchup-stained menus, I was intrigued. My wife, fearing this would not be a classic breakfast by any stretch of the imagination, was not impressed. The food, of course, confirmed her expectations rather than mine. This was rock-bottom cooking at rock-bottom prices. When we passed the site where the diner had stood for years (the building recently demolished), I voiced some mild regret that a landmark had gone. My wife's more objective reply was that she wasn't surprised.

Similar in style, at least from the outside, I found the Thomspon Diner after alighting from the Number 7 subway line in Queens while visiting the temporarily situated Museum of Modern Art. MoMA, as it's known to all, is currently undergoing a huge refurb in its West 53rd Street base, and occupies instead the former Swingline staple factory in Long Island City, Queens. As you descend the steps from the elevated railway track (the subway line has emerged above ground at this point) you're confronted with the low-slung electric-blue building of MoMA, there on the north side of which stands the diner, on Queens Boulevard.

Sitting down at the Thompson, I immediately noticed that the ham, two eggs, hash browns, toast and coffee was $3 (£2) cheaper – about half-price – compared to what I was used to paying in Manhattan, and the food was good. I guess that the thing with 'breakfast' diner food, like someone once said about a naughty child, is when it's good it can be very, very good, but when it's bad it's horrible.

My yardstick, on which I make such admittedly subjective judgements about diners, has for some years now been the Red Flame on West 44th Street, just a couple of doors from the Algonquin Hotel. That block of 44th, between 5th and 6th Avenues and near to the Theater District, includes a number of good and very popular – though not particularly cheap – hotels, including, as well as the Algonquin, the Iroquois, Mansfield, Royalton and the trendy City Club.

Consequently at any time after 8am you'll find the Red Flame full of tourists who are staying at the hotels on the block, and doubtless from further afield, often outnumbering the local working folk. But most importantly, the Great New York Breakfast can be found here, as long as you don't mind ignoring the cholesterol cost. It's eggs with everything, and mostly fried – though you *can* get fresh fruit, healthy cereal and so on if the GNYB isn't your mission.

Certainly the most celebrated diner of the classic mould left in New York City is the Empire Diner, a spectacular 1929 Art Deco stainless steel and plastic affair over on Tenth Avenue at 22nd Street. Again I trudged with my wife across block after block to make breakfast there, but this time we both agreed the trip was justified. Significantly, the menu of this 24-hour eatery isn't dominated by the GNYB anymore, but features all sorts of additions and variations that cater for the late-night after-theater crowd or early-morning after-clubbers.

Nevertheless you can, at a respectable 9am in the morning, still sit down to what for me is one of life's simple pleasures: two eggs 'sunnyside' with corned beef hash, orange juice, toast and jam, and as much coffee as you can drink.

Dining, as opposed to breakfast in a diner, can be a tricky business in New York. 'Hang on,' I can hearing someone shouting, 'Isn't this the eating-out capital of the world, where you can find any possible cuisine on earth, day and night…?'

Well, yes, but with great quantity, quality doesn't always follow. The sheer proliferation of places to eat in Manhattan means that the likelihood of finding somewhere mediocre is far greater than the off-chance of getting somewhere really good, though the latter are certainly there, by the hundred. It's a question of knowing where.

Take Chinatown, for instance. Now, I'm sure there are some amazing restaurants tucked away in the maze of streets north and south of Canal, but my experience – admittedly on a hit-and-miss basis – has only revealed the opposite. I've simply never had a great Chinese meal in Chinatown. To be fair, the same could be said of Hong Kong, where visits to several highly recommended 'regular' eating places were markedly disappointing, although the best Chinese food I've ever eaten was in a hotel restaurant in Kowloon, overlooking Hong Kong harbour.

It seems a bit like that in New York, where some of the best – like the yummy-though-pricey Chin Chin on East 49th Street, the less expensive Shanghai-oriented Tang Pavilion on West 55th and fabulous-for-feasting Shun Lee Palace on East 55th – are in a different league to the average Mott Street chop suey and noodle place.

Pizza's another. Although you are supposed to be get better, more 'genuine' pizza in New York than anywhere in Italy, there's more than a 50:50 chance of getting a deeply boring deep pan if you're not careful. The ubiquitous worldwide pizza chains haven't helped of course, or the hundreds of simply mundane outlets that proliferate across the City.

Having said that, like diner fare, when it's good, the poor people's food from Naples is very, very good. There's a difference between just eating pizza in New York and eating a New York pizza. 'Gimme a slice' is the basic order, but apart from the familiar round pizza, the rectangular thick-crust Sicilian is another great favourite. The real New York pizza is a work of art, and places like John's Pizzeria on Bleecker Street and Lombardi's (which was America's first pizza place, opened in 1905) on Spring Street, though sometimes tending towards a tourist clientele rather than locals, do offer the genuine experience.

Hamburgers, even more than pizzas, are available almost everywhere, at street stands, as a staple of every bar's 'pub food' menu, in diners, and inevitably in the big fast-food chains. Places specialising in hamburgers tend to do them best, like Hamburger Harry's in the Theater District on West 45th Street, serving large juicy mesquite-grilled burgers with a wide choice of toppings and enormous (even by New York standards) salads.

Another favourite among aficionados, many of whom claim it serves the best burgers in town, is the Corner Bistro on West 4th Street in the West Village. Its low prices, good beer selection and 4am closing time have made it a long-standing haunt of the local bohemia. And out in Williamsburg the aptly-named Diner, not a diner in the classic sense though fashioned from a refurbished railroad dining car under the Williamsburg Bridge, serves possibly the best burger in Brooklyn.

At the other end of the gastronomic spectrum, fine dining can be equally a challenge. There are scores of great-sounding places that come and go with fashion, trend-driven eateries that are in with Pacific Rim, out with New American and so on. The long-established are probably the most reliable places. Like Balthazar in SoHo with its Parisian ambience and classic brasserie food, or the more modest and lesser-known Jules Bistro in St Mark's Place, another place for good French cooking. If it's non-pizza Italian you want, you can't do much better than the Trattoria del'Arte up on Seventh Avenue opposite Carnegie Hall at 56th Street.

And some of the trendy joints manage to stay open long after they – or their food – has ceased to be flavour of the month, among them Odeon in TriBeCa which is rightly famous for imaginative good cooking, the Union Square Café where it's almost impossible to get a table without booking a week ahead, and the already legendary Gotham Bar & Grill in the East Village on East 12th Street, where you can experience the very best in New American *haute cuisine*.

The other great gastro adventure in New York is the deli. There are literally thousands across the city, mostly take-away places where you can pick 'n' mix ingredients for the sandwich of your dreams. Some have modest eat-in facilities, and a few – like the celebrated Katz's Delicatessen on East Houston Street – do as much sit-down business as 'to go'. Already well-known before the famous scene in *When Harry Met Sally* when Meg Ryan enjoyed more than just the food (following the film, the napkin dispenser at *that* table carried the hand-written sign: 'Hope you have what she had. Enjoy!') Katz's strictly kosher nosh house serves pastrami or corned-beef sandwiches to die for, but don't even go there if you don't have a big appetite.

Similarly, the pastrami sandwiches at the Carnegie Delicatessen in the Theater District are considered among the best, but of the most celebrated delis there are three that are food emporia on a grand scale. Top of the range is the chic Dean & DeLuca at the SoHo section of Broadway, where a dazzling array of foodstuffs has the taste buds quivering as soon as you step inside. It's a visual feast too, so even if you can't afford some of the far-from-cheap goodies, just browsing is an experience in itself.

Some miles further up Broadway, between 80th and 81st Streets on the Upper West Side, Zabar's is considered by many to be New York's greatest foodstore. The choice of cheeses, coffees, cooked meats and sausages, smoked fish, salad, freshly baked bread and pastries is astonishing, as are the cooked dishes to take away. Plus upstairs there's a great range of kitchen utensils. A one-stop shop for the home cook's every need.

Zabar's long-time rival is Balducci's in Greenwich Village, a family-run store, which has been compared to an ever-unfolding cave with a series of alcoves wherein more and more gastronomic delights reveal themselves, and where the range of foodstuffs is as expansive – and spectacular – as its uptown competitor.

One thing's certain about eating in New York City, there's no shortage of opportunity: from Nathan's famed hot-dog emporium out at Coney Island on the Atlantic Ocean tip of south Brooklyn, to Sylvia's equally famous soulfood restaurant in the heart of Harlem; the quaint but enjoyable Café Edison (nicknamed the 'Polish Tea Room' by patrons) attached to the midtown Hotel Edison, to Yonah Schimmel's traditional bagel shop on the Lower East Side. And not to mention the three midtown branches of Lindy's, with their world-famous cheesecake.

7 Gramercy To Union

Right at the bottom end of Lexington Avenue, No 2 exactly, the Gramercy Park Hotel has, as long as I can remember, been one of those places that has 'seen better days'. When I last stayed there, the antiquated US Mail stamp machine, shining and copper-coloured, was still in the lobby, the elevators and reception area of similar jaded vintage. There's been a recent refurbishment, but the piano bar still retains a *louche* charm. Here generations of hotel guests, locals and New Yorkers generally have met in the bar, to the background sound of jazz piano and smoky-lounge standard vocals.

A friend recalled when a newspaper write-up once described the ambience as 'suicidal'. Maybe. It's long been a hangout for rock musicians – as depicted in the film *Almost Famous* – and similarly hip celebs, even those who might be actually sleeping elsewhere. The last time I was there, Kate Moss and team (the model was probably not a guest, the crew probably were) seemed happy enough. Debbie Harry lived at the Gramercy for a while and, in former times, the elite who regularly stayed at the Gramercy included Humphrey Bogart – whose first wedding took place there in 1926 – and the Kennedys, including the very young John F Kennedy.

A diversion for anyone interested in the history of modern art, just up Lexington Avenue between 25th and 26th Streets stands the 69th Regiment Armory. Home of the 69th Regiment of the New York National Guard, considered New York's only official Irish regiment in the 19th century, it was the site in 1913 of the Armory Show, which introduced modern art to the United States. Organised by the American Association of Painters and Sculptors, the show brought modern painters such as Matisse, Picasso, Van Gogh and Cézanne widespread attention (and initially ridicule), Marcel Duchamp's 'Nude Descending a Staircase' being singled out for particular abuse and parody.

A traditional perk for anyone booking into the Gramercy has been a key to the otherwise private Gramercy Park itself, a classic inner-city garden to which only the residents of the surrounding square have access. Purchased by New York founding father Peter Stuyvesant from the Dutch West India Co in 1651, the farmland was deeded to a freed slave Frans Bastiansen in 1674, the actual park being designed in the 19th century. Leafy and verdant, it enjoys the best of New York's seasons like a mini – but for most of the day empty – Central Park; shaded and cool at the height of summer, picturesque in the snow, a place for street parties and local children at Thanksgiving and Hallowe'en and site of the Gramercy Park Flower Show on the last weekend in April.

CLUB AND PUB

The buildings surrounding the Park, which was built on a former swamp, include some of New York's oldest and finest, replete with history. On the southside these include, at No 16, an 1845 brownstone that houses The Players, a private club founded by the famous 19th-century actor Edwin Booth, whose statue, in the role of Hamlet, stands in the Park. In Booth's day (his brother, incidentally, was John Wilkes Booth, Abraham Lincoln's assassin) the area was the centre of the City's theater world, and The Players was set up specifically to serve the needs of elite members of that profession. Prestigious members have included Mark Twain, the Barrymore theater dynasty, Frank Sinatra and – somewhat surprisingly – Winston Churchill. The club still functions in its traditionally exclusive way, although women were finally admitted to its ranks in the late 1980s.

Right next door to The Players, at No 15, stands the National Arts Club. A grand old building from the outside, the club – founded by *New York Times* art critic Charles de Kay in 1893 'to stimulate, foster and promote public interest in the arts and educate the American people in the fine arts' – is positively lavish on the inside. The façade of the 1840s building was 'Victorianised' in the 1870s by Central Park architect Calvert Vaux, while the interior became a monument to Art Nouveau with magnificent wood-carved fireplaces, stained-glass windows and a huge Tiffany-style stained glass dome, which dominates the ceiling of what is now the bar area.

The walls of the lounges and dining room are covered with works by some of the great names from the club's eminent history, a list that includes – as well as painters and sculptors – no less than three presidents of the United States: Theodore Roosevelt, Woodrow Wilson and Dwight D Eisenhower. Its membership has opened up to other areas of the arts over the years, and includes photographers, film-makers and musicians; current members representing the dramatic arts include Martin Scorsese, Ethan Hawke, Dennis Hopper, Robert Redford and Uma Thurman.

Around the corner, south from Gramercy Park, runs Irving Place, named after the early-19th-century American novelist Washington Irving, most famous as author of *The Legend Of Sleepy Hollow*. Although Irving never actually lived here, this leafy street of charming townhouses does have a literary history as the residence of short-story writer O Henry, who lived at No 55 and frequented the still-flourishing Pete's Tavern on the corner of 18th Street.

One of the oldest pubs in Manhattan – opened in 1864 and vying with McSorley's for the accolade of longest-standing – Pete's is typical of old-established New York bars. Originally called the Portman Hotel, it was bought in 1899 by Tom and John Healy, and it was under the name Healy's Café that it was a favourite hangout of O Henry. With a darkened interior – a legacy of days when drink was frowned upon by certain influential citizens, not to be visible from the street to respectable folk and their offspring – a couple of TVs flicker silently, invariably tuned to a sports channel. The interior has been featured in *Ragtime, Endless Love* and *Seinfeld*, not to mention a few beer commercials. The bar serves good American beers and the house special: large bowls of freshly popped popcorn, free of charge.

The clientele tends to be local residents during the day, with a younger, more 'preppy' crowd in the evening. The bar celebrates its O Henry connection as the place where he actually wrote (in Booth 2 to be exact) – or at least thought up, doubtless while imbibing – his famous *The Gift Of The Magi*.

'O Henry' was the pen name of William Sidney Porter, born in North Carolina in 1862. His life was as colourful as the characters that inhabited his tales. After leaving home to work on a ranch in Texas, he got a job at the First National Bank in Houston. He left the bank after a few years to found what turned out to be an unsuccessful humour weekly called the *Rolling Stone* (!), then in 1895 he began writing a column for the Houston *Daily Post*.

Meanwhile, Porter was accused of embezzling funds dating back to his employment at the First National Bank. Leaving his wife and young daughter in Austin, Porter fled to New Orleans, then to Honduras, but soon returned because of his wife's deteriorating health. She died soon afterwards, and in early 1898 Porter was found guilty of the banking charges and sentenced to five years in an Ohio prison.

From this low point he began a remarkable comeback. Three years and about a dozen short stories later, he emerged from prison as 'O Henry' to help shield his true identity. He moved to New York City, where over the next ten years before his death in 1910, he published over 300 stories and gained worldwide acclaim as America's favourite short-story writer. His time spent in Pete's Tavern and similar establishments clearly took its toll, however: he died an alcoholic with just 23 cents [15p] to his name.

Many years after his death, the name O Henry became familiar to an even wider public as the creator of the Cisco Kid (from his story *The Caballero's Way*). This character became the subject of several Hollywood films throughout the '30s and '40s, and a kids' TV series during the early 1950s. The latter era also saw a series – *The O Henry Playhouse* – based on the author's collection of short stories, which was made for the small screen.

Walking down Irving Place almost its full length, at 15th Street we find Irving Plaza, a contemporary music spot far removed from the world of the National Arts Club or O Henry. A medium-sized venue, its programme regularly features big names alongside lesser-known emerging acts. Since its inception in 1991, the list of star headliners has been varied to say the least, from Billy Connolly to Cyndi Lauper, Iggy Pop to Taj Mahal, Blur to Buddy Guy.

UNION CENTRAL
This end of Irving Place is just a block east of Union Square, one of those
New York environments that feels complete in itself. There's a community
feel about the public space, hosting as it does a colourful mix of folks
walking the dog, students from nearby NYU, buskers, street artists and
people just passing through or hanging out.

From the 1920s onwards, the square became a focus of political
dissent. Like London's Hyde Park Corner it became a venue for soap-
box orators of all persuasions, but also the rallying point of
demonstrations, from the 35,000 unemployed who marched on City
Hall to demand jobs in 1930, to the anti-Iraq War movement of 2003.
Indeed, many have assumed its name came from some link with the
Labour movement, but it was merely an indication of the point where
Broadway met Bowery Lane (now Fourth Avenue).

One of the best-loved features of the square is the Greenmarket,
the most popular of New York's outdoor farmers' markets, which
functions on Mondays, Wednesdays, Fridays and Saturdays. Here you
can browse through an amazing array of fresh fruit and vegetables,
meat and fish, dairy produce and home-baked bread from upstate
New York, New Jersey and as far afield as Pennsylvania. You'll find
straw-hatted Amish farm-folk selling their cheeses alongside Long
Island flower-growers and winemakers from the Shawangunk vineyards
west of the Hudson.

Surrounding Union Square are businesses as diverse as Toys 'R' Us,
Virgin Records and the flagship branch of the mammoth Barnes & Noble
bookstore chain. There's also the Heartland Brewery with its good
selection of premises-brewed beers, the classy Blue Water Grill on the
corner of East 16th Street, which serves stunning seafood and a side
order of live jazz, the even classier Union Square Café on East 16th itself
and the always entertaining Union Square Coffee Shop.

On the corner of the west side of the square and East 16th Street, the
Coffee Shop is a lively bar with a Brazilian-based menu in the adjoining
restaurant. Latin-tinged music adds to the atmosphere, both canned and
from live bands in the bar. The waitresses seem drawn from the stream
of model wannabees who hang out there, located as it is in a district now

The corner of Fifth Avenue and West 52nd, 'Swing Street', once the centre of the jazz universe

Veteran of the Greenwich Village scene Paul Colby at the office of the Bitter End, the Bleecker Street landmark he's been running since 1967

Lach: East Village antifolk promoter, manager and performer in his own right

Ted Gottfried, ukulele ace and proprietor of the East Village music-book and fanzine store See Hear

The building on West 10th Street in Greenwich Village which once reverberated to the sound of the first hootenannies, led by Pete Seeger and Woody Guthrie, launching the folk scene in the 1940s

Williamsburg resident Adam Green of The Moldy Peaches, part of the post-Strokes 'renaissance' of New York rock 'n' roll

The imposingly named Russian Orthodox Cathedral of the Transfiguration of Our Lord in Williamsburg, Brooklyn

The Empire Diner, a classic of Art Deco design and still serving the Great New York Breakfast

Owner Jack Earl from Hackensack, with bar person and the big pig mascot Baron von Swine, outside Rudy's Bar and Grill in Hell's Kitchen

Club pioneer Hilly Kristal relaxes behind his desk at CBGB, the Bowery birthplace of punk which he opened in 1973

Percy Jones, long-time resident of the Spanish Harlem barrio, ex-pat Welshman and fusion maestro of the fretless bass

Pete's Tavern in Irving Place, famed watering hole and one of the longest-established bars in town

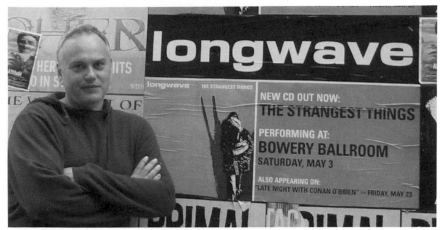

Rob Sacher, proprietor of the Lower East Side music bar the Luna Lounge and LunaSea Records, whose roster includes Longwave

Avant-garde jazz saxophonist and composer John Zorn, a leading light on the early Knitting Factory scene

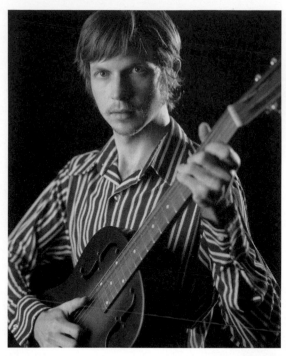

Beck Hansen, one of the first
faces on the antifolk scene,
whose take on folk 'n' punk
broke through via a New York
apprenticeship in busking

Blowin' the blues: a busker
in Astor Place

favoured by photographic studios and modelling agencies. With its tile-and-chrome exterior (like the bar itself) and neon sign simply saying Coffee Shop down the corner of the building, it looks fast, cool and quintessentially New York. A diner-style breakfast doesn't come cheap, but the coffee – perhaps not surprisingly with the South American pedigree – is far better than most.

In many ways Union Square is the hub of the lower half of Manhattan south of Central Park. Just a couple of blocks down from the Coffee Shop you're at the Cedar Tavern, a Greenwich Village landmark, while on the north of the Square is the bottom end of Park Avenue, and that stretch of Broadway that intersects with Fifth at the always fascinating-looking Flatiron Building, New York's very first skyscraper. Walking round Union, you can just feel you're at the centre of things.

8 East Village Others

Everything's relative, even gentrification.

The East Village, despite the much talked-about upscaling of real-estate values and subsequent emigration of homes and business, is still scruffier, funkier, more romantic and tackier (depending on your perspective) than its West Village neighbours. And though new ones might not so easily spring up there, you can still find small independent enterprises that are unique to that part of town.

A walk down St Mark's Place of course, with its tattoo parlours, tarot readers and punk emporia, can confirm one's worst fears of a district having given way to retail touristdom, but since the days of the 1960s head shops, surely it has always been so. As in San Francisco's Haight-Ashbury, even as flower-power idealism blossomed worldwide 30-odd years ago, the anti-materialism of peace 'n' love was to prove a gold mine for someone.

Back in 1966 Andy Warhol's 'Exploding Plastic Inevitable' happenings were stunning audiences at the Dom Theater – now merely a memory at Number 23 – with their mixed-media assault on the senses of light shows, dancers and pioneering proto-punks The Velvet Underground. Indeed, when Warhol and the Factory crowd spied the Dom (Polish for 'home') premises for the first time, the street was dominated by Polish businesses, delis and such. The happenings were a direct forerunner of similar events developed mainly on the West Coast a year or so later, leading in turn to St Mark's very quickly becoming the Village's hippy neo-centre. It even spawned its own alternative paper to the already established *Village Voice*, the *East Village Other*, a publication now revered as a classic in accounts of the US 'underground' press of the late '60s. So by the end of the decade, bells, beads, psychedelic posters and the smell of patchouli oil were everywhere, and so it's been in varying degrees ever since.

And in the streets adjacent to St Mark's life comes and goes much as it has done for the intervening decades since the Village east of Lafayette Street first played host to bohemians as well as bums, with long-standing establishments weathering the storms of the market place-generated by real-estate fixers rather than just plain old supply and demand.

GOING FOR THE 'ONE AND ONE'

We have to go back to 1854 to date McSorley's Old Ale House, on East 7th Street, one of the original Irish-owned taverns in the city. I first visited its spit-and-sawdust interior at the end of the '60s when it was still a men-only bar. Two beers for the price of one (a 'one and one') was the house gimmick to shift more of the amber nectar, that's McSorley's Light or Dark Ale, depending on how sweet you like your beer, and the men-only rule certainly wasn't in deference to some ahead-of-its-time accommodation of the gay community. Far from it, this was old-fashioned macho territory where the bar was a refuge from nagging wives, predatory girlfriends, howling kids and other aspects of monogamous responsibility.

Most bars and taverns operated a virtual men-only policy of course, up until and even after World War II, not just in the US but in Britain and Ireland, where many of them had their origins. Women were expected to use a 'ladies' lounge, and any who ventured into the main bar (ironically called the 'public' bar in most English pubs) were assumed to be of loose moral character or worse. The only difference with McSorley's was that it made it a strict rule of the house – females were actually barred – which it stuck to right up till the early '70s, when it had become a true anachronism.

By that time, this sexual apartheid was blatantly flying in the face of not only more progressive social attitudes to gender equality, but the full fury of the nascent women's movement at its most bra-burning militant.

A hugely publicised sit-in by feminist would-be boozers culminated in their case being taken to the US Supreme Court by constitutional attorneys Faith Seidenberg and Karen DeCrow, and women were finally allowed entry in 1970.

But McSorley's biggest gimmick, that goes right back to its original nomenclature, is that it has only served one drink in its 150-year existence – ale! Even the dark shadow of Prohibition couldn't dim the glow of the golden glory that is McSorley's Ale, the brewery operation simply moving from a few blocks away to the basement of the alehouse itself.

The interior of McSorley's has changed little over the years, the shelves behind the bar stacked high with the memorabilia of decades, the walls covered in New York history. Framed and faded newspapers, like banners, as bold and black as yesterday's headlines, proclaim events as if they had just occurred. Wars, triumphs and disasters; political campaigns and ball game victories; men on the moon; the Twin Towers.

Like much of the story of the Irish in New York, McSorley's was touched by politics, the politics of presidents and protest. Pride of place above the bar when I first visited was a portrait of Erin's most famous American son, John F Kennedy, then only seven years after his assassination amid the green lawns of Dallas. It's still there, dustier than before.

And long before the 'monstrous regiment' of women raised their flag in the bar, the poet laureate of the American left, Woody Guthrie, rallied the early union movement in the back room, guitar in hand.

This was the same guitar, with 'This Machine Kills Fascists' famously emblazoned on its bodywork, with which he helped launch the post-war folk-song revival in the first 'hootenannies' over on West 10th Street in the West Village.

Another celebrated – and oft' inebriated – customer was the Irish writer Brendan Behan, during his time in New York between 1960 to his death in '64. He declared NYC to be his favourite city, and wrote that McSorley's 'has been there for about 100 years and is worth a visit from anybody of any sort, size, shape or creed... The conversation in the saloon is great on New York, which of course these old men do not appreciate now, for they remember the time when the buildings were half the size. They certainly do not appreciate the Time-Life building, nor for the matter of that, the Empire State Building.'

An amusing story regarding Behan in McSorley's was during one of his many (albeit short-lived) bouts on the wagon. He was standing in the bar, with his wife having to stand outside on account of the men-only rule. An admirer approached him, saying he thought his work was brilliant and he'd like to buy him an ale. Behan accepted the drink, which he promptly poured over the floor, apparently as a gesture of protest on behalf of his wife.

The back room is now where a small galley serves up some of the cheapest decent lunch fare in the City, with cheese and crackers and McSorley's famed chilli top of the list.

Weekday around noon the front tables in the bar soon fill up with lunchtime locals, an Irish brogue here, Brooklyn twang there, discernible in the chatter. Others sit alone, reading the baseball scores, scanning the news. A visitor wanders in, greeting friends at a table – 'Found it easy enough' – a Liverpool accent, discussing with the New Yorkers last night's jazz at the Village Vanguard. A barman/waiter comes over with a dozen glasses of ale: no tray needed, a trick of the house is carrying up to 20 half-pint tankards at a time. At two for the price of one, a necessary skill. Business as usual, as always.

'ZINE AND HEARD

Just a block east on 7th Street, a tiny basement houses See Hear. The painted sign announces it clearly enough – a simple depiction of an eye and an ear – but you have to descend the steps off the street to discover it's a bookstore. The name highlights the fact that it specialises in books about music.

Behind a small counter just left of the door, Ted Gottfried quietly presides over his enterprise. Ted opened the shop in 1985 and it's been a fixture there, between First and Second Avenues, ever since. In his native Miami, Gottfried's first business was a record store-cum-bookshop, Open Books and Records – 'I was always into rock 'n' roll' – with four more jobs following before he finally set up See Hear, perceiving a market niche for books and fanzines about music. Rock music, jazz, country – and a lot of punk – all seem to have been written about as much as they've been played. Maybe not the first, or only, but See Hear's certainly one of the few bookstores almost entirely devoted to music.

Opposite Ted's small counter are shelves and shelves of 'alternative' magazines, present-day successors to the fanzine cult that peaked, in his opinion, in the late '90s.

Fanzines, of course, performed their function most perfectly with punk. Indeed, the word itself (in the context of music) emanated from the 1976 New York 'zine *Punk*, editor John Holmstrom coining the phrase for the new underground months before it was taken up by London spiky-heads and their champions in the English music press.

Holmstrom's mag set the standard, with post-hippy cartoonery and 'photo stories' featuring real-life characters on the NY scene: Debbie, Joey Ramone, Patti et al. The Debbie Harry *Playboy*-style centrefold earmarked the peroxide princess as punk's Marilyn, back in the days when 'Blondie' usually referred specifically to her.

You can still buy prized back numbers of *Punk* in See Hear, along with Holmstrom's 1996 anthology of its best bits, including some of the Debbie 'playmate' shoot courtesy of Chris Stein, who took the pictures.

Gottfried sees the decline in fanzines since the late '90s happening from a time when they began to become a 'career move' for many writers and editors, an apparent stepping stone to 'real' journalism, rather than purely being the product of someone's hobby or passion, the spontaneous result of the zealous fanaticism that provided their original dynamic.

Indeed, See Hear was almost a casualty of the explosion of interest in fanzines in the '90s when it expanded to a larger location up on St Mark's Place, offering an even broader array of fanzines of every description. This was boom time, followed, perhaps inevitably, by bust for many. A lot of the new mags were slicker and glossier than their predecessors, throwing the whole economics of 'zines, their distribution and marketing into a spin. The writing was on the wall when Fine Print, the largest fanzine distributor, filed for bankruptcy; some mags went down, retail outlets following them. See Hear managed to survive by closing the new shop and moving back to its more modest East 7th Street location.

Did Ted agree that another reason for the fanzines' decline was the fact that websites might be performing some of the same function?

'Not really, websites are just not the same. They're great for out-and-out-fandom, discographies, pure data stuff.'

We agreed on the inherent limitations of computers compared to books, something the rows and rows of literature, that you could pick off the shelves in an instant, bore testament to.

Among the present-day punk fanzines, the heavy-metal tracts and various other bizarre broadsheets, you will also find what you might least expect: crude (in every sense of the word) publications of the far, far right. Not the 'respectable' neo-conservative Republican right, but the barking mad out-and-out racist right. Not because Gottfried sympathises with a jot of what's in there, but for their sheer entertainment value: 'Because they're more fun than [Noam] Chomsky...and just so insane.'

Ted Gottfried's other great passion is the ukulele. Not the electric guitar, which one might expect of this long-haired rock-music fanatic, but the little toy-guitar-like ukulele. Like all ukulele buffs of course, he's quick to point out it's no toy. He has one lying on the counter, which he picks up and strums with gusto.

His hobby extends to playing as a duo with fellow uke-freak Jason Tagg, calling themselves Sonic Uke. New York and New Yorkers have always struck me as being hot on puns – one of my favourite art forms – and Ted's no exception. The regular jam session open to all comers that the pair host is billed on the sonicUKE.com website as a uke-i-nany.

Now we're on the subject of ukes, he's quick to turn the conversation – me being from the UK (there's a pun there somewhere, but I'll resist the temptation) – to the Northern English entertainer of the 1940s George Formby, who is regarded as something of a god by fans of the ukulele and its near cousin the banjolele. I tell Ted I remember Formby's old black-and-white films from when I was a kid; he's heard of the films, but never seen one, he's simply heard Formby's records. To him, the movies are the stuff of legend.

Pause for thought: I'm in the East Village, talking to a guy who specialises in rock 'n' roll books, punk fanzines and rabid skinhead racist rags (for laughs), about a grinning, slightly gormless pop star (and Formby was certainly that in his day) of my parents' era, whose Lancashire hot pot of a repertoire included such classics as 'When I'm Cleaning Windows' and the double entendre-rich 'Little Stick Of Blackpool Rock'.

Ted goes on to tell me about the house where they hold the uke-i-nanies, where he lives in fact, over on the bit of West 10th Street that dips southwest after crossing Sixth Avenue. That same house was the scene of those very first hootenannies that Woody Guthrie organised with Pete Seeger back in the 1940s, around the time that over in England audiences were roaring to the slapstick-and-song of another working-lass hero, reducing millions to fits of innocent laughter with 'With My Little Ukulele In My Hand'.

Bidding Ted farewell, I make my way over to the address on West 10th, in Greenwich Village proper, just to take a look. The narrow three-storey building also houses a resident psychic in the sub-basement area off the street, advertised in neon on the door. Above are rooms that resounded half a century ago to the musical clarion calls of the American Left, pounded out not on a ukulele but a machine, it was claimed, that killed fascists.

UPPING THE ANTI

If, instead, I had continued along East 7th Street I would have come across a modest looking apartment block between Avenue B and C. Here, at number 207, the poet Allen Ginsberg lived for many years from the 1950s onwards. He shared his modest dwelling with fellow beat writer William Burroughs for a time in 1953, and the famous photo of Jack Kerouac on a fire escape was taken in the apartment that same year.

After the north-to-south Avenues reach First in the East Village, there are three more before you get to the East River, A, B and C, giving the district its local nickname 'Alphabet City'. This was always a tough part of town – in the '70s and '80s the street corners were notorious for open crack dealing in broad daylight – but even this area has seen a change in recent years. It's certainly not what you'd call gentrified or even tarted up, but it certainly feels safer.

It was here I came across one of those puns that New York seems to do so much better than anywhere else, a pet shop called Alpha Pet City, on my way to visit Lach, one of the guiding spirits of the current East Village music scene.

Living on Avenue C, much of his activity is centred on the Sidewalk Café, a bar and eatery on the corner of Avenue A and East 6th, which he has developed as the nerve centre of the so-called antifolk scene. Since the mid 1980s Lach has been a moving force in what he and others see as a reaction to the conservative attitudes that the 'traditional' folk scene had developed over the years. Early antifolk pioneers, including Roger Manning and Cindy Lee Berryhill, heralded a scene that was to include such names as Beck, Ed Hamell and Michelle Shocked, and more recently the Moldy Peaches and comedian Rick Shapiro, the latter one of Lach's protégés whom he rates more than highly.

As well as putting out records on his own indie label Fortified Records by various new names including Shapiro, he's made his own well-received CDs as singer/songwriter, plus nurtured the Sidewalk as an antifolk venue, with its now-established Monday night Antihoots or Antihootenanny giving all-comers a chance to get up and do their thing. He also organises the annual Antifolk Festival in nearby Tompkins Square Park, which lies halfway between the Sidewalk and Lach's apartment on Avenue C, where I got to talk to him at length, first about how he got into music in the first place.

'I was born in Brooklyn which makes me a native New Yorker, and I grew up outside of New York about 10 miles [16km] north of here, a suburb of New York called Rockland County, and I've always been a musician. I was basically born to play music. I started to play piano when I was four or five years old, and was a child prodigy piano player. I loved playing piano; I played classical piano. And I didn't listen to any pop music really. My parents had Sinatra and jazz records and Broadway show records so I heard that, and on my way to piano lessons there was a station in New York at that time called WABC, and they would have the Top 40 stuff so I would hear that on the radio.

'And there was a bit of a confluence of things: I liked playing music, playing piano, and I started writing poetry, and I heard...in '76...I heard

Elton John being interviewed, I guess "Crocodile Rock", around that era, and they said something like he'd just made $15 million [£10 million] in one year, and my ears pricked up, I'm like, "Oh...this piano player is on $15 million for one year", so then they played "Crocodile Rock". And I'm thinking like, "All he's doing is 'da da da da da da, da da da da da da,' and I'm doing these intricate Bach pieces and stuff...he's making $15 million for going 'da da da da da da'?" So that stopped it in the first second.

'The first album I bought was Kiss. Because I was then and I am still now very into comic books, I love comic books. Actually I collect an English character named Dan Dare. Do you remember Dan Dare?'

Do I remember Dan Dare? As a kid I thought I was the biggest Dan Dare fan on the planet. At this point the conversation lapses temporarily as two grown men enthuse to each other about a (very) English comic-book hero, the Pilot Of The Future no less, whose weekly adventures enthralled readers of *The Eagle* 50 years previously...

'Anyway, I heard on the radio [Kiss's] "Rock 'n' Roll All Night", a very catchy song. And I went to the store and I saw the album cover and they were all super heroes, so I thought, okay I'll get that. So that was the first album I bought but I listened to it and I didn't like it. When you're playing Bach and Beethoven, that stuff doesn't really hold up to it. So I gave that record to my friend and didn't think about pop music again until *Sixty Minutes*, the TV show, one of the longest running news shows here in America, on every Sunday night.

'They're usually breaking stories like "Indiscretion of a Senator" or something like that. And they did a story on "Coming Next – the Punk Rock Phenomenon from England". And I was like, "What's that?" And it came on and they had the Pistols, The Clash, The Damned, they had pictures of people dancing and choking each other, and Dave Vanian came out from The Damned, in Dracula makeup, and my parents were horrified and so that made it even more intriguing to me. And they called them musicians, they referred to The Clash as musicians, and they showed a picture of them, and I was like, "Wait, that's not the way musicians look" – I'm classical, used to dressing up nice – "that's really cool, you get to dress up like that and be a musician?"

'And the sound of it, the energy, it just really intrigued me. So I went out the next day and bought the first album I ever bought and kept, which I still have somewhere, which was The Sex Pistols, *Never Mind The Bollocks*. And I put that on and just...the sound of Steve Jones's guitar coming out of the speakers, I was like, "Oh my god". I bought The Clash, The Jam's *In The City*, The Stranglers' *Rattus Norvegicus...*'

British punk, of course, had already been predated here in New York, but Lach admits he simply wasn't aware of any of that at the time. It was the English punks that led him into exploring rock 'n' roll music, delving back into its history.

'I fell in love with this stuff: the Pistols, The Clash. And I was very fortunate, I was playing piano, so I started writing songs and found out very quickly that I was a songwriter. And I started going backwards and learning about other songwriters; there's no other real school for songwriting other than the history of rock 'n' roll. So I picked up Dylan and Phil Ochs, and just started listening to anything I could.'

Inevitably, this led him to The Beatles.

'I listened to the Pistols before I heard The Beatles...but it was like, "Oh, The Beatles are the songwriters", so I listened to The Beatles, and that was basically how I got into stuff.'

What followed sounds equally inevitable.

'I started my first band and it was about time to go to college and I didn't want to go to college, but it was army, school or work, and school was the better of the choices. I got a scholarship so it didn't cost anything; it was basically room and board and the chance to do copious amounts of drugs without having to have any responsibility.'

'I went to school for a year and basically during that year I just taught people how to use hallucinogens properly, and then I dropped out of school for a year and lived in Las Vegas with my friend Norman who became a guitar player, and bass player Geoff Notkin. We became fast friends and we dropped out of Boston University together and moved back to Rockland County and got a house there where we started a band which was called Proper Id – like "Proper ID" you get in the clubs – but we just called it Proper Id. So me, Geoff and Norman and two other guys, John and Mark, who are guitarists, we started this band Proper

Id, and we started playing CBGB's then; that was like 1979/1980. The band would break up and get back together and break up and get back together. We broke up and I moved to New York City.'

It was his move to Manhattan and the conclusions he very quickly drew about the existing 'folk music' scene there, that was to be the catalyst for the whole antifolk thing. Perhaps naively imagining that the live folk scene in Greenwich Village was open to new voices and new ideas, he soon realised that the conservatism that had shunned Bob Dylan when he 'went electric' all those years ago was still rampant among the self-styled folkies.

'I read a Dylan biography and they talked about how he played the open mic at Folk City. I was like, "Wait, that's just a block away from here," so I got the *Village Voice* and I saw they were still having open mics there. So I went there, but they did not love me too much.

'What had happened in Greenwich Village back then was that when Dylan went electric he left a lot of the folkie people out, and they were not too happy about that, and they sort of circled their wagon. They said, "Look, we're never going to be Dylan or Hendrix or The Beatles, but our bread and butter is in this thing called folk, so we're going to call ourselves folk and that way we leave this little bit of real estate in the record stores, like these bins are gonna be ours." You know, sort of Tom Paxton, Joan Baez, so they started this thing called folk, which was not really what I considered folk.

'Folk to me is like traditional music that goes back hundreds of years. You don't know who the author is like Japanese folk music, Irish folk music; it's from the people, it's got a simplicity to it, it's from people at a certain time.

'That's not what I was hearing from these people who were at Folk City who said they were folk. They were saying they *were* folk and I'm *not* folk. I was playing acoustic guitar, they were playing acoustic guitar, they were folk but I'm not folk. Why am I not folk? "Well, you play too fast and too loud, and you know, you curse and you're obnoxious." I'm basically doing The Clash on acoustic guitar, but my own songs. I was being sort of tolerated at these clubs and occasionally kicked out…but there was a bunch of like-minded people who were my age and felt the same way I did, so I'd be hanging out in the alley behind the club with like 30 other people, playing our acoustic guitars, getting drunk, and we had as many people kicked out of the club and hanging out with us as were going into the club.'

Lach's first venture in response was to set up an alternative venue on the Lower East Side, on Rivington Street. This was in the days when the Lower East Side wasn't the user-friendly area it is now, a decade before it was trendy to hang out on Ludlow Street.

'It was an 800 sq ft [75 sq m] loft space. I gutted it and I put in a stage. I slept on the stage during the day and at night I ran a club. And I called it the Fort. It was originally called the Hidden Fortress – there was a movie by Akira Kurosawa, the Japanese director, called *The Hidden Fortress* – but everyone called it the Fort, so it became the Fort. And it was an illegal after-hours club. In New York you have to stop selling alcohol at 4:00am, but people still wanna go out. My club would open at midnight and stay open to, like, half four to noon the next day. And it was a haven for the punks and the misfits, and everyone who got kicked out of everywhere else ended up at my club.'

And it was at this precise moment that the term antifolk was coined, and indeed the whole antifolk thing began.

'The week we opened they were holding the New York Folk Festival, the same people who were in the West Village...just the boring folky guys, so I ran an Antifolk Festival, so that's where the word first began, the Antifolk Movement.'

The club lasted for about a year and a half, during which time, Lach recalls, the scarier side of street life on the Lower East Side was sometimes only too apparent.

'It was extremely dangerous. I had the Colombian dealers on one corner and the Dominican drug dealers on the other corner. So I invited one gang in one night – it's called tagging in New York, it's spray painting – to help "decorate", so now I was in with both gangs and I was like the weird, skinny white kid that they just got a kick out of, so I sort of had gang protection.

'But it was still really scary. There was a lot of violence and drug dealing, but that's why the rents were cheap and as a result the artists were going there because the rents were cheap...you'd walk down the street and there'd be a Keith Haring canvas that Keith had just done; it'd be like glued to the side of a building. It was dangerous but it was very exciting, very artistic, and on Rivington Street at that time, there was a number of clubs – the No Say No, there was an after-hours place called Nickleback – and you'd go to these clubs and they'd be avant-garde and cutting edge, and everyone would be getting wasted...'

Hassles with the local police could be a problem. One night they raided the place, but the cops happened to be Irish (a strong possibility in New York) and there was someone singing Irish folk songs on stage at the time. The officers grabbed a beer, looked around and left the place alone. But eventually the law couldn't ignore Lach's illicit drinking den any longer, as its publicity and popularity increased, so the cops gave him two weeks to shut down.

The venture became what Lach refers to as a 'mobo' (mobile) club for a time, so there would be 'The Fort at Sophie's Bar', 'The Fort at Nightingales' , 'The Fort at Chameleon' and so on, but it was at Sophie's Bar, on Avenue A, that things really started to take off. It was from her appearances on the Fort nights at Sophie's that Michelle Shocked shot to prominence, drawing attention to the antifolk movement in the process. Lach recounts an amusing story about when Bob Dylan visited the club:

'It was a big thing... But what was funny was that the week after Bob Dylan came down Matt Dillon, the actor, came, and someone on stage was doing a song that they had written that week called "The Night Dylan Came" and Matt thought it was about him, thinking, "I just walked in the bar and they're already singing songs about me."'

Antifolk was starting to take off, with Lach promoting various new names as well as his own music, via the Fort events and then deals with record labels.

'Roger Manning and Kurt Kelly got signed to SST records...so that was the first antifolk signing. They were playing the kind of music that we got kicked out of everywhere for, and all of a sudden got signed to a major punk label, and that was very exciting.'

Things were really moving for the whole scene, but it wasn't without its ups and downs for Lach.

'Meanwhile the Fort was moving around: we were at a club called the Chameleon, late '80s, '89. At that point, Paleface got signed by Danny Fields who had managed The Ramones and Iggy Pop. And then there was a group called The Washington Squares, and they were sort of pseudo-bohemian; they would dress up like '50s Beatniks and wear berets and striped shirts and do old folk songs but with a rock 'n' roll beat. They got signed to Goldcastle, and Goldcastle was owned by Danny Goldberg who was managing Nirvana and Bonnie Raitt – and then he signed me.

'So I thought, "Here we go…I get to move onto the next level now," and I put together an album called *Contender*.'

Disaster struck, however, when within three months the label went bankrupt, just as Lach was about to embark on a tour to promote the record. As he later recalled:

'I had thought that would be my ticket, yet within a matter of weeks, my record deal went bust, my girlfriend left me, and I lost my apartment. If I had a dog, it would have died. I was a walking bad country song.'

He decided to move out to San Francisco, just to get away from the New York scene for a while, leading a totally different lifestyle as construction worker by day, playing music at night. But the performance wasn't in front of an audience, it was purely done alone, in his apartment.

'I would write out a set list, I'd light all my candles, I'd take my glasses off so that things were sort of fuzzy and I'd play just to my candles. And I would get such a pure joyous feeling just from the physicality of making music. And I'd lost that feeling because antifolk in the mid to late '80s had gotten to the point where we were "discovered", and everyone found fame and fortune, and the gigs became about who's in the audience, what can this person do for you…and you forgot about the music. I was still getting my joy from the songwriting, but the actual performance wasn't really fun anymore, and I rediscovered the joy of just playing while I was out in San Francisco.'

Lach's daily routine before going out to work on the construction site at six in the morning was to listen to a local oldie station on the radio – 'They played The Beach Boys and The Beatles' – over his daybreak coffee, a routine that was to lead to Lach's return to live performance, recording and the antifolk scene.

'The DJs were really funny and they were going off about Hillary Clinton, and the fact that Chelsea had to fax her homework to Hillary because they were campaigning; this was during the first campaign. So a friend of mine had lent me this four-track and I wrote a song called "The Hillary Clinton Song". And I recorded it on a four-track using pots and pans and my drums and stuff, just to learn how to use a four-track player and have fun.'

Lach sent a copy of the song to the two DJs, just for their amusement, not expecting them to play it, it being an oldies show. To his astonishment a couple of days later they started playing the song, not just once, but throughout the day.

'I called them, "Hi, my name's Lach."

'And they said, "Oh, we wanna talk to you!"'

So they interviewed me on the air and they were getting all these requests, and they asked if the Clintons had heard it yet... I said I didn't think anyone was ever going to hear it. They suggested I send it to Little Rock. So I sent it to the NPR station, the National Public Radio station in Little Rock, Arkansas. And I called them a week later and they said, "It's our most requested song, we play it all the time".

The immediate result was a deal Lach struck with a guy called Hobart who had heard the Clinton song and was interested in managing him. During the year or so of this arrangement, they put out a record with 'Hillary Clinton' on it, released just before the first Clinton election when it was heard on over 600 stations countrywide during election week.

'The night Clinton won he was in Little Rock, and he came out onto the steps of the Little Rock Courthouse to accept the nomination and of course all the Little Rockians were out there, on live TV, and I'm sitting watching it, and he said, "I'd like to introduce my wife Hillary."

'And the whole crowd started going, "Hillary, Hillary," like my song.

'And I was like, "Oh my God, they're chanting my song." So that was cool, and *Entertainment Weekly* picked up on it and did a story on it.'

Around the same time Beck, an alumnus of the antifolk scene, started to make it big, getting a lot of publicity, and a friend tried to persuade Lach to come back to New York on the strength of that. Feeling sufficiently encouraged to get back into the music world in some capacity or other,

Lach decided instead to take a trip to Europe to promote *Contender*, the rights to which had reverted to him when Goldcastle went bankrupt.

During what was intended to be a brief stopover in New York on his way to Europe, for a family celebration marking his mother's 60th birthday, he dropped into the Sidewalk Café to visit a friend who was bartending there. One thing led to another conversation-wise, resulting in the owners offering him the opportunity to start up the Fort again in the back room of the bar. They said he could have full control, with a new piano and a good PA system, starting the next day.

Despite his initial reluctance – 'You know, I'm only in New York for a coupla weeks, but I could always use the extra money' – Lach has been there ever since.

'When I first started there, I was basically doing everything. I was doing the booking and the promotion...and so the scene was discovered again.'

Crucial to this regeneration of antifolk as a continually developing thing, nurturing new talent in a way that the old folk scene had ceased to years before, was Lach's instigation of the Monday night Antihoot or the Antihootenanny, which he considers to be 'the heartbeat of the antifolk movement'.

'It's standing room only, completely packed...that's where the new blood comes in, that's where people who have been on the scene might come back to try out a song...and that's where we discover the new people.'

Then, in the mid '90s, Lach decided to start his own record label: 'I started a label called Fortified Records, and the first thing we put out was a compilation album of antifolk artists recorded live at the club, based on the Monday night. It was called *Lach's Antihoot/Live From The Fort At Sidewalk Café*, like you were there.'

Next came Rick Shapiro, a stand-up comedian whom Lach describes as 'the Lenny Bruce of our time'.

'I discovered Rick, he was playing somewhere else and I said, "You gotta come to Sidewalk," so he started doing weekly shows at Sidewalk, and I couldn't get anyone to write about him. So I decided he's gotta have a record out. They recorded him live at the club, I produced it, and we took four nights and boiled it down to a live record called *Unconditional Love*. And we put that out and it got rave reviews, it got written up everywhere from *Penthouse* to *Billboard*, just fantastic. He's pretty X-rated, but he's brilliant. A New Yorker, a hard character.'

The Shapiro CD was the second release on Fortified, the third was Lach's own *Blang!*, by which time the label was enjoying full national distribution including the all-important big chains: HMV, Tower and Virgin. *Blang!* received some very favourable reviews, including one in *Billboard* that described it as 'a wholly enjoyable voyage into a strange and brilliant musical mind'.

The next Lach 'discovery' to grace the Fortified catalogue after playing the Sidewalk was Major Matt Mason. He'd already appeared on the *Lach's Antihoot/Live From The Fort At Sidewalk Café* compilation album, and his debut album *Me Me Me* was also licensed to an English label, Shoeshine, owned and operated by the Teenage Fanclub drummer Francis Macdonald.

This English connection was just one of several that were symptomatic of a new, high-profile interest in New York bands manifesting itself in the UK at the time, but which impacted more immediately on Lach in that he ended up doing the first of several live tours there.

Major Matt's UK licensing more or less coincided with the emergence of The Moldy Peaches as the next 'new thing' to create a record-business buzz via the Antihoot and regular dates at the Sidewalk. They were soon to be signed by Rough Trade Records, who also signed up Jeff Lewis, another Sidewalk protégé, and The Strokes, who caused the biggest media furore of all on the other side of the Atlantic.

Suddenly, there was a big thing going on in England. Lewis, the Peaches, Major Matt all had albums out, the Peaches were opening up for The Strokes on tour, and Major Matt went over there too. Lach decided, 'I'm going to England.'

'So I did my first of four times over there, and the first time there I played 12 shows in about a week, then I went over again and did just London. Then I got signed to the Agency Group who handle The Strokes and The White Stripes, and I licensed [his third album] *Kids Fly Free* to Track Records. I did a three-week tour, solo, from Aberdeen down to Cardiff... I played Liverpool, at the university... '

At this point Lach breaks off to proudly show me a pair of Cuban-heeled Beatle boots he bought while in the Fab Four's hometown. 'They're licensed by Apple, these are the real thing…Italian leather, they're actually quite comfortable, so I bought two pairs.' His small one-bedroom apartment is full of such souvenirs and memorabilia: comic books, sci-fi pulp magazines, his prized collection of Dan Dare ephemera, an Action Man-style figure of Lach himself, which appears on the cover of *Blang!*.

'While I was doing that tour I played Lincoln, and the guy who ran the club, Steve Hawkins, he was involved with Inspiral Carpets and a lot of people in the business, and we just hit it off…so he said I should come back with the band next time. My band is now me, on drums there's Billy Ficker who was in Television and also in a group called The Waitresses. And Roy Edroso on bass, he was in a New York punk band called The Reverb Motherfuckers. It's just a trio. And the power of weirdness is that I'd just sent an e-mail over to England, to my fan base over there, saying, "Look, I'm coming over to England with the band, we don't have a van, we don't have a tour manager, we don't know what we're doing, but Track Records wants to put out a record and we're coming over to tour, hell or high water we're coming over, so if anybody has any ideas or knows where we can get a van, let us know 'cos we don't know what we're doing."

'So like a week later I get this call, from Steve, saying, "When you come in, have you got work permits, when you come in at the airport?"

'I said, "Oh, I guess the booking agent's taking care of that."

'And he said, "All right, I just wanted to make sure of that… I'll pick you up at the airport, we'll go back to Lincoln, I've got a rehearsal studio set up, so you can get used to the equipment I got for you."'

Steve Hawkins had imagined the e-mail plea for a road manager had been addressed solely to him, rather than all the other folk on Lach's UK mailing list. Whatever, the tour, which was towards the end of 2002, went ahead with Hawkins as tour manager, and the band pronounced it a great success, not least because of his timely intervention.

'So when the tour was over I said, "Steve, the tour's over. We don't need a tour manager any more, but if you want to manage us…"

'And he said, "Yeah".

'So I said, "Great, you're my manager. That's the end of the meeting?"

'And he replied, "That's it, that's the end of the meeting."'

The immediate plan was to take Lach's first three albums from the States – *Kids Fly Free, Blang!* and *Contender* – pulling the tracks from each record to create a new album, *Up The Anti*, and get licensing and distribution in the UK and Europe, followed later in 2003 with an album of new material.

So on the live front, Lach found himself plenty busy, but still finding time to get as inspired as ever with new talent – as usual, via the Fort – which he invariably sees as artist potential for Fortified Records. When I spoke to him, in the late spring of 2003, the label was about to release a CD by an outfit called Testosterone Kills, a gay male couple who aren't afraid to refer to their sexuality in their songs, one playing synthesiser, one on guitar: 'sort of The Clash meets antifolk'.

'I think their stuff is really important because although in New York, in the East Village, it's very liberal, gay rights and stuff, but I'm sure there's 15-year-old kids in Iowa who think that they're the biggest misfits in the world, and to hear something like this done with rock 'n' roll joy can be important.'

Just the night before, Lach's current 'discovery', an 18-year-old called Nellie McKay, had done a sold-out gig at Joe's Pub, a theatre-club venue on Lafayette Street, to which I'd tried to get in, to no avail.

'Yeah, it was crazy, we never thought it would do that well...'

Lach has spent all morning taking calls from record companies who were at the show, with two majors very interested. He enthuses about this latest signing to Fortified.

'Nellie shows up at the Antihoot like so many people before her, and at two in the morning gets up, plays a song and disappears. I think, "Who was that?" The next week, the whole night I'm thinking, "Is she going to show up again, this mystery creature." Three in the morning she shows up again, and gets up and plays...

'I suggest she does a whole show and she says, "Well I've only got those two songs."

'So I say, "Well, we've gotta write some more." And then, within two weeks, she had written another six or seven songs, and every one of these songs is as good as Gershwin, it would make Elvis Costello go "Shit".'

Nellie's demo CD certainly bears out his enthusiasm, a mix of sophisticated-sounding songs distinguished by quirky angular chord sequences and knowing lyrics, vocals delivered with jazz-confident timing and perfect pitch, and an assured piano style that sounds classically trained. It's Ricky Lee Jones-meets-cabaret *chanteuse*, but very much for the 21st century.

She is only Lach's second management signing (the first being Ricky Shapiro), and his instinct has also been born out by her subsequent signing to a major deal with Columbia Records for an album which was due out in autumn 2003. And some rave press reviews confirm it still further: 'She looked like a 1940s movie star, banged the piano like a whirlybird, sang like Doris Day and penned couplets as divine as Cole Porter's said the *New York Observer* , while the New York edition of *Time Out* spoke of 'one of New York's most intriguing performers. She is a dynamite piano player and pitch-perfect vocalist. Stylistically, McKay is like a living, breathing 'White Album'. She will knock off your socks and steal your soul.'

Putting the potential stardom of Nellie McKay into perspective, Lach sees his life as being reasonably focused, the excitement surrounding his latest find just one of the various strings to his bow.

'It gives you a little sense of what my life is like… I run Sidewalk Café, I do the promotion and booking, seven night a week, I run Fortified Records, and I'm married…(a job in itself)…so it's just like my life is very thick, and robust, and filtered and such…just like the City.'

We get round to talking about the City, the East Village in particular, and the changes – economic and social – which have been perceived as both a blessing and a curse by those closest to them.

'There's been gentrification without a doubt…but the end of the East Village as it was, for me, was August 1988 when Mayor Giuliani entered Tompkins Square Park and the rioters were the police…' He's referring to a now-notorious incident when the authorities emptied the Park of 'undesirable elements' in its 'cleaning-up' campaign.

'It wasn't the people, the police rioted, the guys with the guns went on a riot, beat up everybody, that was really the nail in the coffin for me. It's funny, it's 2003 and you'll get some yuppy saying, "The East Village has really changed since 2000."

'And I think, "No. It was over ten years before that." Also in the 1980s, crack and AIDS hit New York, and decimated a large part of the creative population. A lot of people moved out, gentrification came in. Part of the city gets taken over by the artists, the artists make it hip, so the people who want to be near the hipness move in...'

I suggest the process has almost become a law of nature.

'It seems so...for me, after the Park, to complain any more is like complaining about the weather. Here it is, it's happening.'

This is a process that now extends out to now-fashionable areas in the outer boroughs, like the Brooklyn enclave of Williamsburg.

'Williamsburg has become a hip centre...for me when I go over to Williamsburg, it's very cool in a way, but in the same way it's almost prefabricated *cooool* like, "We've made it cool..." You know there's gonna be a lot of coffee drinking, people are going to have the right sideburns you're supposed to have that month, there's going to be the sort of bohemian spot where people are going to read sort of "edgy spoken word", and all that's cool, but on the other hand...'

'What might be interesting is when the babies that are being born over there, when they rebel against their parents, see what they bring to the table. But I don't want to sound as if I'm putting down Williamsburg, I think it's fine...the more places there are for people to play and be cool, the better.'

One of the reasons venues and such have moved, of course, is that it's simply more difficult to run a business in Manhattan, or to a degree anywhere in New York City.

'It's very very hard to run a music venue in New York City right now, the war on terror post-9/11 made it near impossible, then the events after that, the economy going down, then the worst winter we ever had...it was so cold for so long, people were just not going out...the war, the weather, the economy, and now the no-smoking ban that Bloomberg has just put in.

He sees the latter as a self-inflicted complication, which the City will come to regret. 'It's completely insane. It's really wild how Americans will say, "America's the freest country...the pinnacle of freedom." I mean, have you been to Amsterdam? You can smoke pot and get a hooker...'

But, European flesh pots notwithstanding, Lach has a passion for New York, and his slice of New York in particular, that permeates most of what he does, and which is summed up in an opening announcement he sometimes makes at the Antihoot.

'"Hi everybody, you're at the Sidewalk, the coolest club on Avenue A (actually we're the last live music club on Avenue A right now), Ave A the coolest part of the East Village, the East Village the coolest part of New York City, New York the coolest city in America, America the coolest country on Earth, Earth the coolest planet in the solar system, this is the coolest solar system in the galaxy, so you're in the coolest club in the galaxy..." and I say it facetiously, but in some ways it's true...this is *New York*.'

He emphasises those last two words as though to underline the richness of implication in them. Although he's in many ways part of the fabric of this part of town, certainly the musical fabric, and a time-served East Villager, his voice lays bare the sense of awe that the City has inspired in generations of its citizens, and continues to do so.

9 On The Bowery

For the non-American – especially of the generation to which I belong – place names in the United States are imbued with a romance that goes beyond words, conjuring images rooted not in reality but in the cinema and, to a lesser degree, the mythology of music. And this is no more true than in New York. Broadway and the Bronx, Harlem and Fifth Avenue – the very sound of the word Manhattan – all have a value, a weight, that's far greater than mere geographical reference.

In the earliest years of the 1950s, when I was nine, ten or eleven years old, and television wasn't yet common to every home in the country, I probably went 'to the pictures' an average of three times a week. This often amounted to a total of six films a week: most main attractions, unless they were super-long epics, were supported by a second feature, 'B' movie.

One such second feature, actually a series of second features, that was hugely popular with kids at the time involved a gang of teenagers billed as The Bowery Boys. Headed up by the wise-cracking 'Slip' Mahoney and goofy 'Sach' Jones – played in the 40-odd films by Leo Gorcey and Huntz Hall – the five street-savvy youngsters were actually hitting their 30s by the time the series ended its decade-long run that had begun in the mid 1940s.

Their adventure-comedies involved tangles with local mobsters and adult authority, delivered with lots of New York slang and loads of slapstick. Set in what purported to be a tough side of town, this was my first acquaintance with the name the Bowery, and for years after I assumed it referred to a district rather than an actual thoroughfare.

Running diagonally south from the East Village as a continuation of Fourth Avenue, through the Lower East Side and Chinatown, the Bowery, like Broadway, follows what was once an old Native American trail. Historically it was famous in the first part of the 20th century as an entertainment centre, a hub of the American version of the British music hall – vaudeville – and its seedier cousin the burlesque revue. Interestingly, up above St Mark's Place between 10th and 11th Streets on Second Avenue stands St Mark's Church-in-the-Bowery, traditionally spelt Bouwerie, built in 1799 on the site of Peter Stuyvesant's farm. Stuyvesant, one of the founders and first governors of New York back in the 17th century when it was part of a Dutch colony and called New Amsterdam – the British renamed it New York when they took over – is buried in the graveyard there.

But by the time The Bowery Boys were making the name familiar to ten-year-old film fans across the same ocean that the likes of Stuyvesant had sailed, the place itself had deteriorated drastically. By the mid 1950s it had become a byword for skid-row, with alcoholics, drug addicts and other homeless street-dwellers literally living on its sidewalks.

I was made acutely aware of this, again via the movies, in a 1956 documentary *On The Bowery*, which I watched in a Liverpool 'art-house' cinema in 1958. The grainy, ultra-realist *cinéma vérité* film by Lionel Rogosin followed a group of alcoholics with the aid of hand-held – and sometime hidden – camera work. Shocking in its time, it revealed the sordid side of New York City far more graphically than the grittiest of Hollywood fictions.

It was another 11 years before I would see it for myself, and by the late '60s the Bowery – at street level at least – had improved little from the nightmare environment of Rogosin's experimental movie.

By this time the East Village and Lower East Side generally was becoming the area of choice for creative souls who couldn't afford the West Village any more, with painters in particular taking advantage of cheap loft spaces ideal for apartment-studios. I was visiting, with a painter friend, the London-born 'super-realist' artist Malcolm Morley – at the time he was working on his now-famous postcard-based canvas *Racetrack (South Africa),* which he finished in 1970 – who had one such space on the Bowery.

Getting to the entrance to his building from the corner where a taxi dropped us involved that staring-ahead-and-walking-swiftly technique necessary when being accosted by out-of-it characters on city streets, not to mention stepping over bodies that could have been dead or alive for all we knew. A long way from the world of Slip, Sach and the rest of the gang.

Nowadays of course, like much of New York, the whole of that most notorious stretch of the Bowery east of Lafayette Street has been 'cleaned up', a euphemism for the get-tough policy adopted by the City administration back in the 1980s. It was certainly a move that made the streets safer and more agreeable in many instances, but it also threw the baby out with the bathwater when it came to dealing with some of the unfortunates who were displaced as a result.

Now, apart from several missionary organisations that still cater for the down-and-out, there's little evidence of how the Bowery was at its lowest point. Not that it's particularly smart. Like most of the Lower East Side, it retains its hard edges and always will: a rough diamond that no amount of polishing will completely soften up.

UPLIFTING THE GORMANDIZERS

Back in 1973 things were still very much as they'd been for decades at ground level. The artists had moved into the lofts, but there on the street the dereliction was, as always, a deterrent to the kind of new enterprises that have sprung up since, be it shops, clubs or cafés. But it wasn't a deterrent to Hilly Kristal, when he decided to take over the derelict Palace Bar at Number 315 in '73 and turn it into a Country, BlueGrass and Blues venue. He even named it after those initials: CBGB.

I approach CB's, as it's often known colloquially, from Bleecker Street, the club with its trademark black and white awning situated near the corner with the Bowery. Underneath the CBGB logo is the almost-as-familiar OMFUG, which Kristal has decoded in interviews a thousand times.

'That's more of what we do. It means "OTHER MUSIC FOR UPLIFTING GORMANDIZERS,"' he explains on the CBGB website. 'And what is a gormandizer? It's a voracious eater of, in this case, MUSIC.

A lot of people believe that OMFUG stands for something dirty, but the truth is, I felt CBGB sounded so pat that I wanted something to go with it that sounded a little uncouth, or crude.'

The front door is open onto the Bowery though the place is closed: it's midday and hot. Hilly Kristal is sitting behind his desk near the entrance. This 'office' area is archetypal punk: predominantly black walls, smothered in layers of posters, graffiti and band flyers. I laugh out loud at a business card featuring a cartoon monkey with a spiky haircut and leather jacket: the band are called Furious George.

Greeting me, Hilly offers me a bottle of water, before first explaining how he decided the Bowery needed a club in the first place, though what kind of a club, he wasn't entirely sure.

Already a veteran club proprietor – he'd run the legendary Village Vanguard jazz joint in the 1950s – Kristal decided the burgeoning art colony in the area could make the Bowery something of a destination if the venue got it right. He was a jazz fan, but recognised there was a lot of other music around that, like jazz, could attract a big enough crowd to make it work.

'My original idea was for country, bluegrass and blues. Because, the '60s was, aside from of course rock, The Beatles, the Stones, there was other stuff...and I had a lot of friends, musical people. I knew a lot of people it seems were on the jukeboxes. You know, you had country music or you had folk; Dylan was doing folk. But then you had bluegrass, that was getting popular, and you had country blues, city blues. It was all an amalgamation of this kind of music. It was from acoustic into electronic stuff, and I liked it. It wasn't my only favourite music, I liked jazz and classical, but I just felt...especially with the big art colony when I came over...we were at another place, and when we came over here there were a lot of artists on the Bowery, Lichtenstein, Rauschenberg, a whole lotta people.

'So, I knew a lot of people who played, so that was my intention. But what happened was, first of all there weren't really enough people to make it work, enough things to keep it going day after day after day here on the Bowery, which was a little bit different to how it is now – it was a mess.'

The club opened in December '73. The first bands to play there included The Con Fullum Band from Maine, country-folk artist Elly Greenberg and a street group called The Wretched Refuse String Band. None of this clicked box-office wise, any more than the jazz combos he also tried out to pull the punters in.

However, the short-lived problem of what *would* draw sufficient custom was solved in a way that neither Kristal nor anyone else could have possibly predicted. Via a chance encounter with Tom Verlaine and Richard Hell of the nascent punk outfit Television, Kristal tapped into a whole new scene, a scene, far from what he'd anticipated for his club, which was as much about a different style of musician as it was about a different style of music.

'There were all these kids and they had no place to play their own rock music. It was like a resurgence of new rock, only because they were young people who had their thing to say. They weren't interested in '60s rock, they weren't interested in folk or anything, they were interested in their thing, what they had to say.'

Hilly had been approached by Television's manager Terry Ork, who persuaded him to book them into the club, although he had second thoughts as soon as they started playing. Admission was just a dollar [60p], and the band attracted a meagre crowd, half of whom were non-paying friends: 'They not only didn't pay admission, but didn't have any money for drinks.'

But it was the music that completely floored Kristal, with its screeching guitars, ear-splitting volume and cacophonous delivery. He'd never heard anything like it and didn't want to again. And certainly not in his club.

Ork, however, was persuasive enough to get Hilly to book them again, along with another new hot rock band from Forest Hills in Queens called The Ramones. Deciding he had nothing to lose, Hilly agreed – especially when Ork assured him the new outfit had a big following. Of course, they didn't have: not many more turned up than for the earlier debacle. As for their music, Hilly thought they were worse than Television: 'The most untogether group I'd ever heard'. With equipment that kept breaking down, their set was a total shambles.

And out of this chaos – appropriately many would say – was born punk, though at the time the term had yet to be applied to this new music and the attitude that went with it. And it was the attitude as much as the music, the do-it-yourself spirit, that inspired Hilly Kristal to encourage the bands by providing a place to play when few others did.

'They played in their lofts and basements, there were a coupla places where they could play once or twice a week, but nobody would let them play their own music really most of the time, so when I saw this, I just kinda let them play, and then because there were so many of them I said, "There's a change in the policy, the only way to play here is you have to do your own music." And that started people coming around, I mean not customers too much but the musicians...everybody wanted to do their own music. Some of it was terrible, and others worse than terrible, but it was interesting.

'It's very interesting when people are allowed and encouraged to just do what they feel, it doesn't matter about anything else. You know this was a recession, but things were pretty reasonable. I bought a truck and did art moving and all kinds of things to support it; this was not making money, it was in deficit. And I thought if I was a singer and writer, I would have wanted something like that. So that's what happened, I was nurturing it, and helping...and it was fun.'

The CBGB website carries a colourful account by Hilly Kristal of what it was like running a rock club on the Bowery back in the 1970s, worth quoting here at some length:

'Having a rock club on the Bowery, under a flophouse (believe it or not), does have some advantages:

1. The rent is (was) reasonable.

2. Most of our neighbors dressed worse than, or more weird than our rock 'n' rollers.

3. The surrounding buildings were mostly industrial and the people who did live close by didn't seem to care too much about having a little rock 'n' roll sound seeping into their lives.

'The disadvantages: within a two-block radius there were six flophouses holding about 2,000 men, mostly derelicts. I would say most of them were either alcoholics, drug addicts, physically impaired or mentally unstable. Some of the men were veterans from the Vietnam War on government disability, and others were just lost in life or down on their luck. The streets were strewn with bodies of alcoholic derelicts sleeping it off after two or three drinks of adulterated wine reinforced with sugar. There were lots of muggers hanging around on the Bowery preying on the old or incapacitated men. When people were let out of jail or institutions they were very often housed in one of these flophouses by the city, so we had to deal with these crazies trying to come into the club.

'Mostly, knives were the weapon of choice. By the time things improved around here, I had collected over three dozen knives and other assorted weapons. The muggers – or "jack rollers" as they were called on the Bowery – were not as dangerous to ordinary people as they seemed. They were used to picking on the old men or others who were completely out of it like three sheets to the wind.

'The Bowery was, to repeat, a drab, ugly and unsavory place. But it was good enough for rock 'n' rollers. The people who frequented CBGB didn't seem to mind staggering drunks and stepping over a few bodies.'

CBGB's became the prime venue in launching the punk revolution. Hilly even gave The Ramones a residency later in 1974: 'After a while I was persuaded to keep putting them on, and they started to get better. I still don't know whose idea it was, but when they started doing the 17 minutes of music – 20 songs in 17 minutes without stopping – it became interesting.

'We didn't call them punk, they did after. Television was the first band of that genre, as you know. And then came The Ramones, The Stilettos – who, after someone split from the group, became Blondie – Patti Smith of course, Talking Heads, The Shirts and Mink DeVille. And each one was very different from the next, you know. You take all those bands and none of them sound like the other.'

I pointed out that when the punk thing happened in London, a couple of years after Television and The Ramones first hit the tiny CB's stage, the opposite was true. The bands, by and large, did sound similar to each other, more formula-driven. I suggested there wasn't as much pure originality as with the New York outfits. Hilly's view was that English punk, the punk of The Sex Pistols and The Clash, was more a reflection of the society young people found themselves in during the late '70s, as in fact it was with some American punk scenes that began to emerge in more 'post-industrial' cities.

'I think that in London there was an anger, there was a lost feeling... From what I remember, especially in the '70s, you had the same problems there, that young people had no place to go, they felt they were going to live on the dole, there was no future for them, and it was an upsetting thing. And the same here in certain areas...when The Dead Boys came from Cleveland, I think they typified the London people. Cleveland was a place where there used to be almost a million people and it was down to 600,000 people: people were leaving, there was nothing going on, and that's what they wrote about, "Ain't Nothing To Do". There was nothing for them, so Pere Ubu, The Dead Boys...Devo was a little different, but they were angry. And Detroit was another.

'But that was just part of it, there were all kinds... Boston had some wonderful bands... Boston was a good place, and even the radio stations there actually played the new music: BCN played new music. Here they did a little bit, but not much. And it spread to other parts of the country.'

Also prior to the UK punk explosion of 1976, Hilly was responsible for another milestone in the birth of the genre when in the summer of '75 he organised a Festival of the Top 40 Unrecorded New York Rock Bands. He put it together as a response to the prestigious Newport Folk & Jazz Festival which had relocated to New York City in recent years after being an annual event in the social calendar of Newport Rhode Island since the 1950s. It was written up in the *Melody Maker*, one of the very few instances of the UK music press taking notice of the new music emerging from New York.

'There was a Folk & Jazz Festival, it was called the Newport Festival, it used to go on in Newport, Rhode Island. And Newport got tired of all these kids coming up to this very ritzy place, so they pushed them back into New York, so then [the promoter] George Wein had it in New York. When I saw this was happening, I thought, "Boy, everybody's gonna be here, so I'm gonna have my own festival of all these things." And I started advertising the day their festival started.'

Hilly took out huge ads in the *Village Voice*, the *SoHo Weekly News* and a New Jersey music paper called *The Aquarium*, listing the 70-plus bands who would be appearing at CBGB's festival, catching the attention of fans and journalists who were in town for the Newport bash.

'I timed it so that we advertised during their festival, so everybody came to New York and saw these big ads, all these bands listed they'd never heard of, they were like, "What's going on?"

'So a week after, the next week, we had our festival, so a lot of the writers stayed around, and everybody stayed around, just to see. They'd never heard of these bands, they didn't know. So it worked, it really worked. There was a lot of interest and everybody started coming down, so it was good, and it was a very exciting time.'

The '75 Festival was a launch pad for a number of names-to-be, including Television, The Ramones, Mink DeVille, Tuff Darts, The Miamis, Johnny Thunder And The Heartbreakers, and Richard Hell's post-Television band The Voidoids. It was also the biggest event yet in the progress of punk, a scene developing beyond the doors of CB's. What up till then had been called 'street rock' had now become 'punk rock'. Other venues like Max's Kansas City started featuring the new bands and in January '76 John Holmstrom launched his magazine *Punk*.

Bands from all over the country started to ring CBGB's for bookings, and the music industry itself began to sit up and take notice, with A&R men checking the club out almost nightly. Seymour Stein of Sire Records was one of the first off the mark, signing The Ramones and arranging a UK tour to promote their debut record. It was this that Kristal sees as the 'wake-up call' the British press needed, to look more closely at their own burgeoning punk scene.

'Of course, I think that when The Ramones went over there, and they [the UK bands] were doing the same thing, I mean they were playing in all these pubs and nobody cared, but then *NME* and *Melody Maker* and *Sounds* said, "Well, The Ramones are having success...our bands are great too, so let's write about them..."'

Through 1976 and '77 as punk's influence was being felt worldwide, CBGB enjoyed the kind of celebrity status that few clubs do. The disco-heaven of Studio 54 up on West 54th Street did for a while, but the closest parallel that springs to mind is that of the Cavern in Liverpool in 1964, in the wake of The Beatles and British groups generally taking rock music and youth culture by storm.

A visit to the club to see what it was all about became a must-do for anybody who was anybody. Some – like singer Linda Ronstadt who fled after five minutes – didn't like what they heard. (Ms Ronstadt had briefly got an earful of The Ramones.) Others, like Allen Ginsberg and painter Jean-Michel Basquiat, became regulars.

CBGB was also fertile ground for other new sounds as well as in-your-face basic punk. The new-wave bands that followed in the wake of the first-generation punk outfits, quirky groups like The Cars and Talking Heads – and Debbie Harry's post-Stilettos line-up Blondie – brought a more melodic pop dynamic to the hard-edged assault of the musical angry brigade.

Over the years, hundreds of bands have set up on the graffiti-covered stage at CB's, and towards the end of the '80s Hilly Kristal branched out into the place next door. CB's 313 Gallery concentrates on acoustic-orientated acts, plus poetry readings and such. Underneath in the basement there's CBGB's Downstairs Lounge, another space dedicated to either acoustic-based music or the occasional experimental and jazz performance. And, as the name suggests, it also functions as a gallery for art, something Hilly has always been keen to encourage, a cross-fertilisation of the arts of one kind and another.

'It's a gallery, and every month we have a new showing of new artists. We don't make money out of the art, but it doesn't matter, they sell. And then we have more acoustic or lighter music: different kinds of music. We also have a lounge downstairs where we have parties and some rock things, and also on a Sunday jazz... We used to have poetry, we still have poetry once in a while; across the street now is a poetry club where they have it all the time. Thirty years I've had poetry, since right at the beginning. A mixture of poetry, writers, art and music, especially rock.

'Warhol used to be in here all the time, Andy Warhol used to have a place half a block up, and everybody, poets and artists, was together. I'm glad they're there, they seem to be doing pretty well; it's really about having your say, and a lot of poets, a lot of artists, are also musicians.'

Hilly seems content with the way things are. He's still booking bands in every night of the week, though he admits there isn't quite the same buzz as when it was all so new. 'It was a lotta fun, those years. And now – we have some good bands, but anytime at the beginning of something, you're working hard, working day and night, and you're finding so many new things... I wish it could happen again...I guess it happens all the time, but I'm old.'

He also welcomes most of the changes that have occurred on the Bowery.

'I think it's great, I mean upstairs, for instance, instead of being a flophouse, they rehabilitate people who have been on drugs or have just lost the point, that's what they do upstairs.

'Across the street we have a designer studio, and some nice restaurants – and we still have some old restaurants with fireplaces. And they're building next door to us – an NYU building, it's a dormitory, and it's kinda busy – I don't think they come in, but I don't know if they come in, I can't tell if they come in or not.

'You have what I call real people, not people staggering up at eight in the morning to get a quart of Muscatel for 40 cents [25p] a glass: that's how it was.'

10 East Side Stories

The Lower East Side has always had a reputation as a tough, gritty neighbourhood. Even The Bowery Boys were originally cast as the East Side Kids in their early movie exploits, while 'serious' accounts of the area's gangland history have ranged from Sergio Leone's 1984 epic *Once Upon A Time In America* to 2003's *Gangs Of New York*. The former film traced the Jewish 'mafia' through generations of crime spanning the first half of the 20th century. The latter was Martin Scorsese's much agonised-over evocation of the bloody baptism of the City as represented by warring Irish gangs in the middle of the previous century.

The Five Points, which is the geographical hub of the action in the Scorsese film, no longer exists as such. Located in what is now part of Chinatown, it was the junction of Park, Worth and Baxter Streets and is now at the southernmost tip of Columbus Park. The area is the *de facto* southern tip of what came to be known as the Lower East Side, years before Yiddish, Italian and Chinese communities changed its ethnic complexion completely.

More recently the whole district north of Chinatown up to East Houston Street, like its East Village neighbour on the other side of Houston, has undergone changes driven by fashion and real-estate prices rather than by the traditional, indigenous population.

Attracted by affordable rents, the Lower East Side was the latest – possible the last – district in lower Manhattan to become the 'new bohemia', with an influx of creative talent and associated enterprises. This trendification had its inevitable consequence of course, the now-fashionable area in turn becoming out of the financial reach of the next wave of musicians, artists, writers, whatever. But for the moment, the legacy of the last decade or so is there to see in shops, bars and most importantly as far as the musical community is concerned, live venues.

OFF THE BOWERY

The Bowery Ballroom isn't actually on the Bowery, but just around the corner on Delancey Street. Delancey, which runs east from the Bowery right to the Williamsburg Bridge, gets an honourable mention in that most honourable of songs, Rodgers and Hart's 'Manhattan', the evocation of a 1920s New York that never really was:

'It's very fancy, on old Delancey
Street you know,
The subway charms are so,
When balmy breezes blow,
To and fro...'

The building that houses the Bowery Ballroom was completed just before the Wall Street Crash of 1929. Before that the site was occupied by a three-storey theatre, typical of the district.

During the pre-World War II years, Number 6 Delancey was occupied by various retailers: a jewellery store, a haberdashery, then a shoe shop, which stayed there until the 1970s. After that, the store-front was a lighting showroom and then a carpet store until, in 1998, it became the Bowery Ballroom.

Described by one ecstatic journalist at the time of its opening as 'a cool-hunters wet dream', the seven-month transformation into a 500-capacity three-level rock club managed to retain much of the Art Deco detail in an otherwise state-of-the-art music venue. Brass and iron metalwork adorns the mezzanine area, the basement on the other hand is best described as grungy. Another opening-night review seemed most taken by the drink rests fitted next to the toilet-paper dispensers in the bathrooms.

There's a feel of a classic 20th-century elegance about the place, albeit 'shabby chic', offering a level of comfort combined with a great sound missing in a lot of rock venues. When I looked in, a broad-based roster of up-and-coming attractions included local hot names French Kicks and Longwave, ex-Bunnyman Ian McCulloch, '80s chanteuse

Suzanne Vega and antifolk scene graduate Michelle Shocked. Plus the latest rave on the block – from Denmark, actually – The Raveonettes.

The Bowery Ballroom was a second-venue venture on the part of the proprietors of another Lower East Side music spot, the Mercury Lounge. Located at 217 East Houston, between Ludlow and Essex Streets, it occupies the ground floor of a building that was a restaurant – Garfein's – in the early part of the 20th century, then for no less than 60 years, from 1933, a tombstone retailer. There's still evidence of the macabre trade in the club. The large, foot-square wooden beams on which monuments were displayed, was used in the construction of the Lounge's street-front window. And apparently there's a tombstone embedded in the end of the bar's counter top, though when I was there, it was too crowded for me to search for it.

From the start, the aim of the club owners, in their own words, was simply 'to build the best sounding room possible and book it well, and to provide all musicians who come through the room with quality production'. In terms of the sound quality, they certainly succeeded, the brick-walled music space and high-tech system providing one of the best club listening environments in the City. And you can see the bands unobstructed from just about any part of the room.

It was at the Mercury Lounge that the much-acclaimed (and, some would say, much hyped) Strokes got their first big break. The booker for the club at the time was Ryan Gentles, and when he heard a demo tape of the band he was hooked – so much so that within weeks he was managing them. Aided by his enthusiasm, the buzz about The Strokes began to build, and Gentles soon seemed to be devoting more time to them than to booking acts into the Lounge. He subsequently quit his job there, but not before securing his protégés a weekly residency, which helped raise their profile even further at a crucial point in their career.

ASTORS' PLACE

Many years ago, long before tombstones were being touted on the premises, the Mercury Lounge building once housed the servants of the Astor family, and was connected to the Astor mansions up on Fifth Avenue by a series of labyrinthine underground tunnels.

The Astors were the original New York aristocrats. John Jacob Astor was an early tycoon – not to mention notorious slum landlord – who became the city's very first millionaire. In 1827 he purchased some land for a farm; 30 years later his sons built two mansions on the site. The Astor mansions soon became the focal point of the city's *nouveau riche*, high society flocking to Mrs Astor's grand social events, usually held in the elegant ballroom. Eventually one of the sons, William Waldorf Astor, for some reason to spite an overbearing aunt, had his mansion demolished and replaced with a hotel, which he called the Waldorf. In reprisal, the aunt had the next-door property also converted into a hotel, the Astoria.

Soon the hotels were joined together as the Waldorf-Astoria, in the early 20th century the most prestigious address in New York City. When the hotel eventually moved to its present location on Park Avenue in 1929, the previous site on Fifth Avenue at 34th Street was up for grabs again. Within a month the old hotel was being demolished, to make way for the Empire State Building.

SHEER LUNASEA

A dedicated club crawl of the Lower East Side would also have to take in venues as varied as Arlene Grocery on Stanton Street, which features as many as six or seven different bands a night, and must be the only club in Manhattan to feature a punk/metal karaoke every Monday; the Living Room, also on Stanton, which, as its name implies, is cosy, intimate and biased to acoustic acts; Tonic, which while specialising in 'experimental' music, allows that to cover a broad church involving jazz, pop, rock and electronic performances; and the Luna Lounge on Ludlow Street, cutting-edge club and also headquarters for LunaSea Records, both ventures run by a key 'mover and shaker' of the New York underground music scene, Rob Sacher.

The Luna Lounge is a free-of-charge walk-in joint that functions commercially as a bar. Consequently it's the newest young bands that get exposure there, crucially for many. I meet up with Rob late morning; the bar has yet to open. We think about lunch; Katz's famous deli is just round the corner on East Houston, though I know from experience it can be a queueing job, standing in line as the Americans have it (or 'on line' to New Yorkers) anytime around midday. Neither of us are that hungry, so we walk and talk for a couple of blocks north of Houston before settling for iced tea.

A native New Yorker, Rob tells me how, growing up in Brooklyn, he first came across what might be called underground music via the earliest manifestation of The Ramones, when they were playing CBGB.

'I was born and raised here, in the '60s and '70s. I'm from Brooklyn, from the East Flatbush section of Brooklyn, and I grew up in the '70s, and went to CBGB's probably like '76, to see The Ramones, and I thought I was going to see a Latin band. I already knew about Santana, you know, I had some Santana records, and it was a Latin name, so I thought I was going to see something like Santana. It took me like a week to decide whether or not I thought it was utter crap or if I loved it. I mean I was in shock, I couldn't believe it.'

Manhattan – the City as, like all New Yorkers, he calls it – was always very accessible from when he was a child, because his father was a taxi driver. So by the middle '70s, that meant the new clubs of Manhattan.

'I think my first real introduction to what we call modern music today, or the roots of modern music, in '75 or '76, were The Ramones. My father was a cab driver, so I was coming into the City (we call Manhattan the City) ever since I was like four or five years old. I would get a ride, a chequered cab, a big old cab; it was like a tank, and I'd ride in the cab with him at the weekends, he was babysitting me. It would be like the holidays, with my father in the cab, so I really knew New York City. I could get you to Yankee Stadium or the Empire State Building at the age of six.

'But we never rode the subway – you know what you call the tube – so I never used the subway or the bus system, it was always the cab. That was like the family car; if we were going into the City we'd put the light on and if we'd get a fare into the City, I'd hop in the front seat, my mother would be in the front and some stranger in the back.'

Before The Ramones, of course, there was music around for teenagers, but nothing like that. And as it was before they were record stars, what impressed Rob about hearing them for the first time was the very fact that it was live.

'It was before they had a record out. Before that the only music I was aware of was music that I could hear on progressive radio stations; between 1970 and '77–'78 in New York City there were one or two radio stations on the FM dial that played album rock, what we used to call album-oriented rock, progressive rock, that kind of thing, and so at that time I was listening to The Eagles, Jackson Browne, Linda Ronstadt, and of course the British stuff like The Who, Jethro Tull, The Kinks, the Stones, The Beatles, things like that.

'But I draw a real line between what you hear on the radio and what you hear on an album and what you see live. Music starts from the first live band that you see. Everything else is a reproduction of music. But to actually see and hear and feel music, you can only do that in a live experience, with live music as it's being played.'

He warms to this theme of the importance of live music, and how it eventually moulded what he ended up doing with his life.

'Actually the very first time I saw it being played I was probably about seven and I saw a cover band; my parents were staying upstate, about two hours from here, in a bungalow colony. People in the City used to go up to the Catskills, and they would go to these small hotels and bungalow colonies, and they would have like a rec [recreation] room. And I saw a band, they were called The Lonely Souls, and they were a cover band doing all Byrds songs, on a 12-string guitar, and that was the first time I ever heard a band, and that changed my life. I mean hearing a Rickenbacker in a live room, you know for me it was The Byrds, I mean I might as well have been seeing The Byrds – and after that I knew I would either be a musician or I would be close to music, making a living close to music. But the first thing that I really saw that involved an original modern band were The Ramones.' He pauses for a moment to recall, much, much later, another encounter with The Ramones.

'I got to meet Joey actually. I produced a record for Joey many years later around 1990 or 1991. I produced a New York goth band called The Ancients, and Joey heard a copy of it and called me up, left a message on my answering machine. It was really cool, I came home and it was like [cue Joey Ramone impersonation], "Hey Rob, this is Joey Ramone, I heard your Ancients CD, man, I really really like it man, I really wanna work with you guys, so, gimme a call."'

It was one thing being a fan, of course, no matter how traumatic the impact of The Ramones or anyone else, another getting actually involved in the music business.

'Well, I was a songwriter, I had a small deal at Dick James Music, which was the company that had The Beatles publishing early on. But my A&R guy didn't last very long, he was only there for about six months, and as soon as he was gone, I was gone. Nothing I wrote actually got published – it was all sort of like "in the works" – and then when he was gone, nobody was there to follow through with it, so nothing came of it.'

What did follow was a series of self-motivated inductions into various aspects of the music business, that today would be called a learning curve.

'I worked with Harry Chapin, he was a folk singer. I met him and he invited me to a workshop that he had at his house in Long Island, and I went out there once a month for about two years, 15 or 20 times in two years. It was working on the craft of songwriting, that was in 1974 or so. I also took a recording-engineering class, so I had some experience in a studio, a 24-track studio, and I guess I tried different things.'

This was while he was still at high school, during which time he was also with several bands.

'I played guitar and keyboards. Keyboards were actually my first instrument, but I really liked guitar. I went onto keyboards eventually, I sort of made the switch over to it; I'm a better keyboard player than a guitar player. So I was like the side guy. I wrote and I was the side guy in a couple of bands that I played in, this was in high school in '71 till around '76 or so. And then I went to college. I didn't start college till I was about 21 and I had played in bands up until that point, and I decided I really wanted to go to college, I didn't want to miss that opportunity.'

College provided opportunity in more ways than one, in fact it gave him the chance he'd been looking for to get involved in the business in a more fundamental way.

'I ended up on the concert committee, and from there I was in the business – I fell into it. A club [the Sanctuary] opened up that was doing really poorly in the town that I went to school in – the college town – and I walked in and said, "If you let me run the music here, I'll pack the club for you."

'And he had nothing to lose so he said, "Okay". They'd been playing disco music in the club, but there was already a fancy disco in the town with the brass railings and all that kinda shit, and this was '79, so we brought in like punk and new-wave records – all my friends pooled our records together – and we had probably between all of us 100 albums, which was probably half or a third of all the albums that existed in that time, in that genre.'

Rob and his coterie of post-punk poseurs obviously cut something of a dash both sartorially and attitude-wise in the Sanctuary. Whatever, it was his first taste of modest success.

'I mean this predates Depeche Mode: this is '78, '79, '80. And we had our dayglo ties and our fancy going-out clothes from either the punk or the new-wave scene. It was either the Talking Heads or it was The Ramones, but they were kinda like, Blondie, very complementary to The Ramones. You could be there in a leather jacket or you could be there in a white linen jacket with a dayglo tie, straight pants and Beatle boots. And we all came from New York, but we went to school in a hick town, but we were New Yorkers. So it was a huge success right from the beginning, the place had like 200 kids and we had a line to get in all night long.'

From there the route to the music business proper in New York City was an almost inevitable, if convoluted, journey over the next few years.

'I left school to help a friend sell a music magazine. I left for about a year, a year and a half. During the period that I was gone the guy who owned the bar went out of business, 'cos he had no idea of what he was doing, no clue. He actually ended up in construction, which was where he belonged. He called me up and said, "If you come back to New Paltz," which was the town where the school was, "I'll give you the bar, just pay off my debts."

'I said, "How much debt are you talking about?"

'He said, "I've got $25,000 [£16,000] of debt."

'They were actually boycotting the bar for some reason – I don't know what he did but there was a boycott or something – he was out of business, the bar was shut. So I said, "Alright, let me work under your licence for a little while and I'll start paying you $500 [£300] a month," and when I opened it up again there were 300 kids trying to get into the place. I would have been a senior that year so I still had a lot of friends that were there, so it was word of mouth.

'From that moment on I was in the bar business, and because I was in the bar business I was in the music business. The bar business was an opportunity for me to be in the music business. And to be in the bar business closely associated with the music that I'm promoting. I wouldn't own just an old-man bar or something, that would be boring.

'So I owned that bar from '81 to '86 and then the drinking age went up to 21 in New York, in fact the whole country, it went from 18 to 21, put me out of business. I had a few bucks saved – I'd had a small step in between, I opened up a video store for two years – and was able to double my money in two years in the video store.

'So by '88, I came down to New York with $40,000 [£25,000] – and six credit cards – which was enough to open up a store-front bar. But I opened it as a club called the Mission, and it was a gothic industrial club predominantly. But we also did Manchester style, The Furs and so on.'

He eventually sold the bar-cum-goth club, which is still there on the Lower East Side, now called the Ace Bar, to his DJs, but not before he had become well and truly immersed in the cut and thrust of the New York underground music scene.

'The first thing they did was get rid of the DJ booth and put in a jukebox. I was like, "You guys are brilliant!" Now they've split up, but a close friend of mine still owns it. He lives in LA, he's like a writer out there for screenplays and stuff like that, he does editing and screenplays. He still owns the bar, he runs it through the internet, he's got like an internet connection; he can watch the bar on his television at home on the computer, it's very cool. He's got four cameras set up and he can call the bar and say, "Oh, you're wearing stripes today," and give them a hard time. He's great.

'Anyway those were great days. We had the Marychain come all the time when they were in New York, The Pogues were there all the time, we used to have private parties with The Sugarcubes: anyone who was on tour, and they wanted a low-key, out-of-the-way place, you know, not like Limelight. But they'd be playing big places, like they'd be playing the Ritz which was up by 52nd Street at that time, it was a 2,700-capacity room.

'One night the Nine Inch Nails were opening for the Marychain and the show was cancelled because the night before they'd had a hip-hop show that had rioting afterwards, so the fire department came down the following night to raid the club. They missed the night it had happened but they picked on the next night – typical. My friend was actually booking the Ritz at that time and they told him, "If you oversell the show, you're gonna go to jail."

'Of course it was oversold, all the shows were oversold as a matter of course. So they cancelled the show. We had a press party for Nine Inch Nails scheduled for midnight, which was after their opening slot, and the Marychain were supposed to do an after-hours party at 4am. But both of them turned up at the same time, and our room only held 100 people, but we had about 3,000 people trying to get in and there was a line all the way down the Avenue. Pretty funny, we had some fun nights there.'

When he eventually sold the bar to the DJs he took a couple of years off 'travelling', before coming back to New York and opening the Luna Lounge, where he's been for eight years. 'Just a local bar that does local bands,' as he likes to put it.

It was directly out of the Luna Lounge experience, seeing worthwhile bands who for one reason or another didn't have a record deal, that Rob Sacher started his LunaSea record label, the first band to appear on it being Travis Pickle.

'There were some great bands that were regularly playing at Luna, telling me, "We're not getting deals." Travis Pickle is the first band that I did a record with, and they were wonderful. They had a singer named Carla Capretto, and she was adorable, really cute, a really good singer, the vibe was great. They were better than Yo La Tengo, they were more interesting. I mean they could rock; they were a little all over the place, and they were a little like Yo La Tengo – that's just an example – but much better looking and cuter and more exciting, but they haven't got a deal. I heard various reasons why. They even had their own recording studio. One of the members of the band is an excellent producer, he produced the demos that got Longwave signed to East West in the UK and RCA over here.'

To date, Longwave are the biggest name to emerge out of the LunaSea 'stable' of new-blood New York rockers.

Nominated by *Alternative Press* magazine as 'One of the 100 Most Important Bands of 2001', Longwave are often compared by reviewers to Radiohead. Like the British alt-rockers, they're a guitar-oriented band who combine strong melodies with intelligent lyrics. Consisting of front man Steve Schlitz, bassist Dave Marchese, second guitarist Shannon Ferguson and Mike James on drums, Longwave toured the UK with The Strokes, getting column inches of press and wild crowd reactions for their Who-like amp-throwing climax to their set. Asked whether this was the way to being noticed, Ferguson told one journalist, 'Our label wanted us to make an impression, so the A&R guy gave us a $3,000 [£2,000] budget to wreck all our gear. We did, but not so badly. A rental amp, who cares? I just didn't want to smash my guitar.'

They've since toured as opening act for The Vines, and their major label signing confirmed Rob Sacher's view – and initial gut instinct, it's fair to say – that they are simply one of the very best young bands to come out of New York in a long time.

But the mortality rate for bands in what is, indeed always has been, a hard-to-survive business, is high. Bands come and go, burst on to the scene then dissolve, a fact of life particularly apparent to Sacher, whose two business arms – Luna Lounge and LunaSea – are involved with new, upcoming talent. Added to that has been a sea change in atmosphere and attitude as a result of the events of September 11 '01.

'I think what has happened in New York, and you can clearly see with LunaSea, is that after September 11 music really changed. The direction of music really changed. Before September 11, music was going in different directions. There was the music that was popular in New

York from like '90 to 2000, stuff that was sort of influenced by Sonic Youth, Luscious Jackson and such, kind of dark-edged – post-modern I think it was called – stuff that came after Nirvana; it was very serious and doomy. And there was another trend: happy hardy rock bands that were punk influenced, but were much more upbeat and much more positive about the future, sort of like the message was, "We're all going to die so let's just have a great time right now, take a lot of drugs, have a lot of fun and don't worry about the future."

'There was a band called Kitty In The Tree, we put their album [*Hello Kitty*] out and they were a really successful, popular band until September 11. We put that record out a year before, and there's a track called "New City" on it: it's almost about September 11, but it was written two years before. If you listen to "New City", it starts off with sirens and basically it's the message that the band had, that we're all going to die so let's have a good time. But after we survived September 11th, no one wanted to hear that message anymore 'cos they didn't want to think about partying for a while, they didn't want to think about surviving, they didn't want to think about anything but staying inside. It was all *really* doom and gloom then, and with bands like Interpol all the music got completely serious and very introverted.

'And those kind of bands have become very, very successful. They were all around before September 11, drawing 40 people, but the year after September 11 it was a whole new thing. Kitty In The Tree dissolved, another band called Youngster, they dissolved; I never actually put out their record but I produced four or five demos for them. There was a band called The Cogs, they plodded on for a while but they eventually dissolved. They were kind of glamorous, colourful bands, that were exactly the opposite of Longwave and Interpol.'

Out of this post-9/11 milieu, however, it was the more upbeat Strokes that were the first to 'make it' on the bigger front.

'It's kind of ironic that none of those bands were actually the first to break out, The Strokes obviously were the first. They didn't have the happy party attitude, but they really did have a punk following, so it was sort of an amalgamation…they weren't as dark as some of the bands that were out there, but they certainly weren't a happy party band. They were right on that edge, I think that's why they were so successful. Plus they had a lot of support early on, as you know.'

We both agree that The Strokes' success has been something of a phenomenon, particularly in the UK where – unlike New York – they had no track record of live appearances on which to build a fan base. The word-of-mouth hype, in such circumstances almost as important as an orchestrated press-driven hype, was also a crucial factor in the UK buzz surrounding Brooklyn's Yeah Yeah Yeahs. With only an EP in the record shops at the time, their London appearances at low-key venues nevertheless attracted queues round the block when they first crossed the Atlantic in 2002.

But Rob is keener to talk about new names. His fascination – as always, I suspect – is with the next up-and-coming outfit, whether they're going to stay the course, to see if his instinct is right.

'There's an interesting band, I'm gonna be really curious to see how this band does, stellastarr*, who have survived the party thing, they're sort of lighter than the Yeah Yeah Yeahs or The Strokes in general vibe, they're really breaking now, and they're in the UK in about a week or two, they're opening for The Raveonettes. They're a really good band, excellent, great songs, and I'm really curious to see if they're gonna be accepted, you know. They have a great fashion, they look great, they play great, they have great songs, they're great people, but they're just a little lighter than the dark bands like the Yeah Yeah Yeahs, you know, so we'll see.'

Since then four-piece stellastarr* have toured as support to Longwave, made another trip to the UK and secured an album deal with RCA, with a self-titled debut album released in September '03. The press surrounding them when, like the Yeah Yeah Yeahs, they only had an EP to their name, has been ecstatic, London's *NME* enthusing:

'stellastarr* are a dream of a band with nearly every element absolutely perfect. stellastarr* are quirkily creative, balancing unpredictably complex song structures with an unerring instinct for pure pop. This is a band with wit, imagination and a knack for hooks.'

Rob sees the post-9/11 change as partly what he describes as generational. 'It was definitely like BC and AD, you know, Before Christ and After Death, talking about September 11, and anyone who was successful way before September 11 is completely out of fashion now here in New York: Lou Reed, Sonic Youth, they're just gone and it'll be another seven or ten years before they're rediscovered, Luscious Jackson, all those bands from '92 or '93, are dead in the water. They couldn't get arrested now. It's a generational thing, you know. You've gotta be between 21 and 25 to sell records, to be relevant.'

And this is the age group at the Luna Lounge?

'No, I actually skew a little older, I would say the girls are between 23 and 27, and the guys are between 25 and 31, something like that. Late 20s to the early 30s. New York is the only place in the world – London may be like this, I'm not sure – but New York is the only place in America certainly, where you could easily expect people of 30 or 40 to come out on a Friday or Saturday night to go to a bar because they don't have kids, they don't have families.'

Right now in Manhattan, any club owner – indeed, any resident for that matter – is acutely aware of the pressure being brought to both businesses and lifestyle by escalating real-estate prices, a pressure that will see Rob Sacher moving his bar out to Brooklyn in the not-too-distant future. It's a move he regrets having to make; being a native of the borough, he has no romantic trend-coloured view of Brooklyn as the new East Village, Lower East Side or whatever. But needs must.

'Brooklyn sucks, that's the thing. It's the kids coming into the City, they just got here, they don't know any better, and they can't afford to live here. But it's a drag. I don't wanna go back to Brooklyn; it's dirtier, it's industrial, I don't like industrial chic or anything, it sucks, it's grim. And Brooklyn has the highest cancer rates in New York, so you don't wanna go there. Having said that, I'm opening a bar there pretty soon.'

No doubt he'll invest the new venue with the same passion he does the Luna Lounge – though whether it will inherit the name isn't clear – and the record label likewise, which he presently runs from the double apartment on 2nd Street, which he shares with his wife and business. It's a passion for the musical dynamic of New York City that, at the end of the day, transcends any preferences or prejudices about location.

11 Brooklyn Highs

Words like multiracial, cosmopolitan and multicultural come easily to mind when thinking of the ethnic mix of New York, a city born out of immigration and the movement of peoples from all corners of the globe. Wave after wave of the poor and the hopeful, the adventurous and the persecuted, came to this point to disembark, lured by the promise of what lay west across an untamed America, but many deciding to go no further.

The Statue of Liberty, built by Frédéric-Auguste Bartholdi in Paris and shipped piece by piece across the Atlantic in 1886 as a gift from the French people, is famously inscribed with the affirmation 'Give me your tired, your poor, your huddled masses yearning to breathe free'.

Millions took America up on the offer and, as they sailed into New York harbour past the green copper-clad giantess, it seemed that this first port of call was good enough for them. Good enough or, in a lot of instances, far enough; many had spent their meagre savings, pawned every possession, for the actual voyage, and the Ellis Island immigration depot off the southern tip of Manhattan was not only the gateway to the New World but literally journey's end.

Myriad ethnic communities sprang up in the five boroughs, making the city of New York even more attractive to further émigré consignments from Europe and elsewhere, who could now find a ready-made home-from-home community who spoke their language, ate their kind of food, shared their problems. For the immigrant, it was far easier to become an American in New York without losing your 'old-country' identity than in most places across the vast continent to which Lady Liberty beckoned. And for that matter, it still is.

To reacquaint myself with what must be the best view of lower Manhattan and the cheapest excursion in the City, I took the Staten Island Ferry, which serves commuters 24 hours a day, chugging from the South Ferry Terminal near Battery Park to the borough of Staten Island, passing Liberty on the way. For years a modest 50 cents [30p] took you the round trip there and back, and now it's even cheaper – it's free. This way you can see the most popular icon of New York just as the generations of immigrants must have done, torch aloft welcoming them into the harbour. But the most spectacular vista on the ferry ride is that of Manhattan itself.

While Staten Islanders take it for granted as part of their daily trip into the City (people from the outer boroughs refer to Manhattan as 'the City' though it's only one-fifth of it), tourists and other joyriders marvel at the landscape. Traditionally, it's also been a favourite for romantic rides after dark for generations of couples, the eerie black waters lapping silently between them and the lights of the most famous skyline on earth.

It's a skyline that's been changed dramatically by recent events of course: the previous time I took the ferry the view was dominated, by the Twin Towers of the World Trade Center. But even their gaping absence has a chilling familiarity about it; when I first made the trip back in the 1960s, they hadn't even been built.

WALKING IN WILLIAMSBURG

Of all the various immigrant groupings that established themselves in specific areas of New York, the most immediately apparent to the casual visitor is probably the Chinese community centred downtown north and south of East Canal Street in what has come to be known as Chinatown. As Chinatowns go – and most big seaports, from Liverpool to San Francisco, seem to have one – it's enormous, with reputedly the largest Chinese immigrant population anywhere outside Asia. An estimated quarter of a million Chinese live and work in the district – a substantial number illegally – many never leaving the neighbourhood. With its exotic food markets, cheap knock-off designer shops, esoteric medicines and – inevitably – hundreds of restaurants, it's virtually another country, more Macau than Manhattan.

Little Italy, on the other hand, has shrunk over the years. North of Chinatown, the latter has expanded into its streets while the Italian population has been absorbed into the rest of the City and its suburbs. The tight-knit community that flourished between Houston in the north and Canal Street – and the backdrop for innumerable, mostly inaccurate, Mafia movies – is no more, but the area is still good for its Italian eateries and some exquisite delis.

Likewise the Jewish community that traditionally settled on the Lower East Side is now either the stuff of fiction or the history books, but its legacy is still apparent in the hundreds of small businesses that still flourish there. Again it's the food places – the delis, bagel bakeries and kosher restaurants – that are of the most immediate interest to the visitor simply wandering the streets.

One of the ethnic communities whose presence can still be felt in a specific area is the eastern European population – particularly Polish and Russian – centred in parts of Brooklyn. I became particularly aware of this when I took the subway – for reasons more concerned with the scene than the sociology – to the latterly trendy 'hipster' enclave of Williamsburg.

The clash and contrast of the multiplicity of cultures inherent in New York is in your face round every corner: rich and poor, exotic and mundane, ancient and modern. Nevertheless, coming across a monumental 'onion-domed' Russian-style church – the imposingly named Russian Orthodox Cathedral of the Transfiguration of Our Lord – in an otherwise very ordinary, indeed slightly down-at-heel, Brooklyn street, was intriguing. Even more so when, viewing the building from the other side across McCarren Park, I could also see the Empire State Building and the Chrysler Building shining improbably on the horizon, way across the East River.

McCarren Park lies on the border of Williamsburg and Greenpoint, the latter area said to have 'the densest Polish population this side of Warsaw', an observation made by general manager Jon Weiss when the club called Warsaw opened its doors in the fall of 2001. The club's location is another example of cross-cultural fertilisation, housed as it is in the ballroom of the Polish National Home (PNH) on Driggs Avenue, Greenpoint.

The PNH has been serving as a focal point for the local Polish populace since it opened in 1914, providing a venue for social activities, political meetings, charity functions and so on, and is rich in the history of the tightly-knit community. Bizarrely, when Warsaw functions as a rock club, it's in the 'old world' environment of vaulted ceilings and gold-painted walls, with a mural showing the cities along the banks of the Vistula River overhanging its long, long bar.

It was opened by Steve Weitzman, who had been booking bands for a dozen years already, most famously into Tramps, where Bob Dylan and Prince were among the many big names featured. His approach to the home's administrators to annex the 1,000-person ballroom as a rock venue on certain nights was a direct response to the increasingly fashionable status of the area, and it immediately scored with cutting-edge names like Black Rebel Motorcycle Club and The New Pornographers as well as established acts such as Patti Smith.

It's that supposed 'hipness' that came to be associated with the area, now somewhat derided by the ultra-cool, that has drastically changed the character of Williamsburg over the past few years. In actuality, it's yet another instance of the sort of urban flight often instigated by the artistic community, from an inner-city area increasingly out of their price range property-wise, followed swiftly by young professionals eager to move somewhere now-trendy that they can afford.

Walking down Bedford Avenue, which has become the epicentre of this bustling scene, I was aware that what had happened in this Brooklyn neighbourhood relatively recently was the result of a process similar to that which transformed the East Village 20 years earlier. A sometimes confusing process captured by Derek de Koff in an article in *New York Magazine* in 2002 headed 'Down and out in Williamsburg? Not exactly. How the victims of a sputtering economy are fueling a creative explosion', in which he recounted an overheard conversation in a Bedford Avenue coffee shop:

'The girls in question, both wearing choppy cavewoman-invents-scissors hairdos, are halfway through their iced mochas when they embark upon a heated debate as to whether they're living in the old Manhattan, the new Manhattan, or some unconfirmed-as-of-press-time Manhattan. From what can be overheard, there are those who tout Brooklyn as the new Manhattan, and there are those who tout

Manhattan as the new Brooklyn. Whatever the case may be, the old East Village is now the new West Village – despite the fact that Avenue C is the new Avenue A. However, Avenue A is over, because Williamsburg is now the new East Village.'

Passing coffee lounges serving this new café society that stand alongside traditional Williamsburg enterprises like vodka-oriented liquor shops, delis and even a Polish-language laundromat, I browse in a recently established bookshop, coming away with a collection of haikus by Jack Kerouac. Like most of the businesses that have sprung up in the wake of the migration from Manhattan, the shop has noticeboards where people advertise apartments for rent, alternative medicine, lost dogs and, of course, local gigs.

Thirsty in the hot afternoon sun, I decide to pass on an organic juice bar and grab a beer in Rosemary's Greenpoint Tavern instead. You won't find it in my recommended list at the end of this book. The fairy lights festooned round the window looked like a left-over from Christmas, the plastic cups in place of glasses a left-over from a student-union hop, my two fellow customers, nodding off at the bar, just left over.

But it's in the evenings, especially at weekends, that the area really comes into its own, as places like the L Café and Fabiane's coffee shop vie for custom, competing against a number of now well-established music venues.

Just a few blocks west of Bedford, North 6th Street is a focus of musical activity. Galapagos, one of the longer-established venues in the area, features a wide range of entertainment from DJs and live bands to performance art. Fashionable looking with exposed beams and ducts, it was challenged competitively by a newcomer, literally next door, when NorthSix opened in 2001. A big, airy 400-capacity club, it, too, has a broad booking policy from rock to jazz to salsa to folk.

Compared to the vastness of Warsaw and NorthSix (which the *Village Voice* compared to a school auditorium), Luxx on Grand Street is relatively intimate. With reflective wallpaper, plastic tubing and neon lighting, it's been likened to a Coney Island bumper-car ring, a fantasy environment in which local, national and international acts and DJs appear seven nights a week. The club's designer and creative director,

Ebenezer Luxx, said at the time of its opening, 'I saw what was happening from visiting my art friends out here over the years. It's the most creative neighbourhood in the whole country. Williamsburg is a viable neighbourhood and it's natural for music to move out here to it.'

Pete's Candy Store, over on the other side of McCarren Park on Lorimer Street, is – like Galapagos – a venue that's been open for longer than most. It has a reputation as a drinking place (it was nominated as the best bar in Brooklyn in the 2002 *Zagat Survey*) with a live-music policy particularly sympathetic to the musicians' needs. Consequently its modest stage has featured little-publicised appearances by names such as Beth Orton and Loudon Wainwright, who enjoy the room's cosy atmosphere. Owner Juliana Nash, a Williamsburg resident for a decade, gives artists a great flexibility, which they clearly enjoy, allowing them to choose their own set times, and even invite friends to 'sit in' on their act or share the billing if they wish.

The mushrooming of new clubs in the area wasn't just a result of the newly arrived audience being created by economic migration from Manhattan; an increasing number of venues were finding the going harder in the City too, so entrepreneurs like Weitzman welcomed the opportunity to follow the trend to Brooklyn.

And, crucially, those same financial pressures were acutely felt by the musical community itself, a thriving local scene being guaranteed as the burgeoning Williamsburg bohemia included its fair share of musicians, producers and even record-label proprietors.

It was a natural place for Adam Green of The Moldy Peaches to settle, for instance. He left his native Kisco in up-state New York with collaborator Kimya Dawson, after forming the band, which became one of the first names to emerge from the East Village-based antifolk scene. He bohoed in Manhattan for a while, wandering round Central Park, playing in the subway, before taking his chances on the open mic antihootenanny sessions at the Sidewalk Café. Williamsburg was an affordable address for a first place in New York. Green is typical of many.

The scores of other bands who have settled either in Williamsburg or other parts of Brooklyn in recent years include French Kicks, The Mendoza Line – natives of Athens, Georgia – and Oliver Chesler aka The Horrorist.

Like many of the immigrant communities all those years before them, the Poles of Williamsburg notwithstanding, the musical community has gradually spread its centre of activity from Manhattan – which was its original focus for generations – to the outer boroughs of the sprawling megalopolis that is New York City. But, contrary to the apparent nature of this process, can it spread indefinitely?

Whatever, as I walked the relaxed sunny stretches of Bedford Avenue I found myself thinking that the Polish sausage vendors and cafés with their sauerkraut and beetroot soup, along with the National Home and Russian Orthodox Cathedral, will probably still be there, ticking over in their time honoured way, after the coffee lounges and clubs are long gone.

PROSPECT PARK LIFE

And south of Williamsburg, in the leafy streets stretching south of the slightly overgrown Prospect Park is Marlborough Farms, the house (named after a nearby street) that has been occupied in almost hippy-commune style by the musical 'family' of the folk-rock sounding Ladybug Transistor. It's in a quiet neighbourhood, which at the start of the last century was planned as an enclave for those wishing to escape the hurly-burly of city life, and has been a home, recording studio and general headquarters for the band, whose whole attitude and sound can be said to be more rural, folksy even, than most of their contemporaries.

The band is the long-term project of guitarist and trumpeter Gary Olson, who got together with two musicians no longer in the line-up, for their debut album *Marlborough Farms* in 1995. Gigs around the New York area followed and, in 1996, they were joined by brother and sister Jeff and Jennifer Baron (on guitar and bass respectively). They toured Switzerland (!), where they were billed as '*amerikanisches Familienidyll*': 'An Ideal American Family'.

In 1997 their second collection, *Beverley Atonale*, was released on the indie Merge label. Drummer San Fadyl joined the band, with Sasha Bell also coming in on keyboards and flute. The group was growing, as was their reputation. The next year they realised an ambition by collaborating with Soft Machine founder Kevin Ayers on a French re-working of his 1969 classic 'Puis-Je/May I?'.

Their third album, *The Albemarle Sound*, appeared in 1999 to critical acclaim, while a European tour established them in what would be their strongest non-US territories, Norway and Sweden. It was on this tour that they added the sixth member to the band, violin player Julia Rydholm, who now plays bass, Jennifer Baron no longer being in the line-up.

At each stage the band confirmed more strongly their unique sound as inheritors of the jingle-jangle folk-rock tradition that went back to the psychedelia of the '60s, with touches of The Beach Boys and all manner of other ingredients thrown in for good measure. Classical influences were even brought to bear with 2001's *Argyle Heir*, a long way from what was going down among most of the New York rock community at the time.

At the moment, Gary Olson is the only member actually living at Marlborough Farms, but it's still the band's HQ and rehearsal space. All the five-piece group have lived there at one time or another. Olson is a native of Brooklyn, and sees it as the most expansive, least claustrophobic, part of New York City.

'I grew up here in Brooklyn, born in Park Slope. It's difficult to meet other true New Yorkers these days. Brooklyn's huge and I love the diversity. It's a lot more sprawling than Manhattan, so many interesting far-flung corners. Growing up here, I never realised how segregated the rest of the world is in comparison.'

The band, who continue to play Europe regularly, cut their teeth in the clubs of Manhattan of course, but now they are as likely to be playing in a Brooklyn venue.

'Back then it was Brownies, Tramps, Mercury Lounge. Our regular haunts these days are Knitting Factory, Bowery Ballroom, NorthSix and Southpaw.'

A new album was recorded in March 2003 – and released in the fall – at the Wavelab Studios in Tucson, Arizona, the first to be laid down by the band outside their own 'in-house' facility at Marlborough Farms.

The other side of Propect Park from Marlborough Farms lies Park Slope, a comfortable residential neighbourhood where we find Southpaw, a relatively recent club venture on the part of Todd Abramson, who also runs the longer established Maxwell's in Hoboken, New Jersey, just a short ride over (or under) the Hudson from Manhattan.

A spacious two-tiered area with a state-of-the-art sound system, the club has gained a reputation since opening in 2002 as one of the best venues in New York City, with a booking policy mixing local, new and established names that Abramson has already found to be a reliable formula at Maxwell's.

He started at the New Jersey venue as booker in the mid '80s – it has already been open seven years or so – and he is now part owner with Steve Shelley of Sonic Youth and another partner. He's found that the varied programme of attractions has been what people have seemed to like about both venues. When we spoke, his upcoming shows included older acts including Dave Davies of The Kinks and Nancy Sinatra, rubbing shoulders with newer names like Dashboard Percussional and Thee Shams.

Because Hoboken is in a different state, he finds he can often book both clubs in for dates on a particular artist's tour schedule, although some acts naturally go down better in one club rather than the other.

'There's some stuff that will work better over there and vice versa, but I'm also doing a fair amount of touring acts, doing both rooms at the same time, so it kinda works out nicely.'

Todd also runs Telstar Records, an indie label that he sees as an extension of the rock 'n' roll end of his live policy, just putting out material by very new names rather than the broad-based approach in the two clubs.

'Telstar is an instance of, kind of the opposite of what I was talking about where I'm dealing with a pretty small-range focus, mainly rock 'n' roll bands, like the garage bands, the rhythm and blues groups, you know, stuff I can get involved in and focus on that, so that's more of a labour of love. I mean, recently the music that I've been doing for almost 20 years has gotten fashionable, but that's gonna change too, but things have been going pretty well...it's basically a one-man operation, but you have a roster with three or four bands.'

Some of the exotic names with material out on the label include DMZ, The Mummies, the marvellously titled Swingin' Neckbreakers and Les

Sexareenos. As with most indie record ventures, it's seen by bands and proprietor alike as a leg-up to bigger things for the acts. 'I put out a record by The Mooney Suzuki, and they're on Columbia now. Sometimes it happens, sometimes it doesn't.'

And like so many independent promoters, he's the first to admit he got into the business as a fan.

'It was just becoming a very passionate fan of music at an early age, it wasn't something I really planned. You know it's one of those things, you start getting that vibe, like, "Okay, what am I gonna do when I grow up?" And then one day you realise, shit, this is it.'

One Manhattan club proprietor, talking to the *Village Voice*, summed up something of the dynamic that creates 'scenes' like the Brooklyn/Williamsburg phenomenon:

'The hipsters and artists tend to always have to emigrate somewhere else and move to the next cheap, cool neighborhood. In that sense, those venues are kind of chasing a trend or a scene, which is to their detriment probably. But in the short term I am sure they will get their sea legs beneath them, and it will benefit live music in New York.'

12 Lights Out And Other Afterwords

As I was putting the finishing touches to this book, in London in August 2003, the news broke via the broadcast media of the massive power blackout over the northeast United States and Canada, including New York. The images that immediately stuck in my mind were the obvious human ones – people struggling free from stranded subway trains, office workers asleep on the steps of the New York Public Library on Fifth Avenue, the ferry terminals clogged with hundreds of thousands of commuters who would normally take the train, ordinary folk helping direct the traffic – but most telling of all was the fact that, for the first time in many, many years, you could see stars over Manhattan.

It sounds like the title of a Woody Allen movie, but it was true. For the first time since the last big power crash in the 1970s, the light pollution that emanates from every big city, and from this bigger-than-big city in particular, had been inadvertently shut off.

I remember as a child visiting the countryside where there were no street lamps at all, and very little motorised traffic by today's standards, the Milky Way was visible in all its million-star glory. Even in the towns the configuration of the stars and their position in the night sky was familiar to everyone, just by looking up. The only time I've experienced that in decades was on a visit to New Zealand, where light – and lots of other forms of pollution – have still to take their toll.

The television images of a darkened Manhattan skyline were eerily beautiful, although buildings that we always think of as being lit at night suddenly plunged into darkness made it look like some post-apocalypse abandoned city. But what it brought home was how dependent we all are on fragile networks of technological support that we take for granted most of the time, this being particularly true of the modern metropolis. It's not just the neon-lit adverts that blinked off in the blackout, but survival mechanisms on which we depend to sustain our daily way of life, from transport systems to air conditioning, food refrigeration to the television news, hospital equipment to the internet.

What, I began to wonder as I watched the drama unfold, of familiar places on the streets of the city? Would there be candles and bottled beers only at Rudy's Bar, or maybe an acoustic set before the sun went down outside the Sidewalk Café?

Like many New Yorkers it seems, Sidewalk link-man Lach got something positive out of the short-lived crisis. 'I was in Dubway Recording Studios (over on West 26th Street) working on the mixes for my upcoming album with my producer Richard Barone and engineer Al Houghton. Ironically, we had just finished the mix of the song "Power Lies Within" when the power went out! We looked out the window and saw the crowds starting to gather outside so we knew it was more than just our building.

'Naturally, our first thoughts went back to 9/11 and we marched down the darkened steps to the streets. From passing radios we heard the news that the whole Eastern Seaboard was out and that it didn't look like terrorism. We called off the day's session and I sent a psychic message (the phones were all jammed) to my wife, Anu, who was in midtown, to meet me at home. I then joined the sea of people on the streets for my walk back to the East Village.

'We remained without power for 30 hours, the East Village being the last area to be restored. During that time I got to know some of my neighbours better, got further into a marvellous book (*The Amazing Adventures Of Kavaliar And Clay*), started building a Star Trek model that has been sitting on my shelf for 15 years, read some *Krazy Kat* strips from the '30s, and watched a turtle dove build a nest on my fire escape and produce one shiny egg.

'When the power finally came back on, a thunderous cheer went up from the neighbourhood. The last time a collective human outcry from the streets was heard it was the gasp of horror as the first tower went down. To hear this time a cry of joy and relief was marvellous and well worth the wait.'

Likewise, the Luna Lounge's Rob Sacher felt the power failure had its upside: 'The first great blackout of the new millennium left New York City without lights, but in exchange we received for the first time a brilliant opportunity to see the stars and planets that are regularly obscured from our view. People were quite friendly and neighbourly and it made each block seem like a small village with folks looking out for each other. I wouldn't mind if we did this once each year.'

It seemed to be something of a pattern across the City, at least where musicians and their audiences were involved. Shay Visha told me how the Knitting Factory coped.

'We were supposed to have World Inferno playing in our Main Space, but due to the blackout we opened the front bar up. I got some of the interns and other staff to hand out half-price flyers to the masses of people that were on their way home, and then basically we started a street party.'

Despite some often difficult neighbours, on this occasion partying outside the club seemed to be universally popular.

'We had all the neighbours out on the street, hanging out on their balconies etc, enjoying the freedom of drinking in the streets. Two hours into this, the band set up on the road and did an "unplugged" show for all. It was a great atmosphere on Leonard Street that day. We stayed open until they couldn't drink any more.

'At twelve midnight, with a (battery-powered) boombox blasting music in the front bar, I announced that all drinks were now $1 [60p], which I can tell you went down a storm. The party continued until three or four in the morning. My eight staff and I stayed at the club all that night into the morning, and woke up to Bloody Marys for breakfast.

'Nearly everyone I spoke to on the day said that what we did was fantastic, and it reminded them when most of New York was more like that, where you could sit outside and drink, where you could sit in a bar and smoke and hang out all night or day long. With a carefree, free, cool vibe, a happy environment.'

The media, as well as running interminable who-was-to-blame inquests that went on for days after, was full of stories of folk sticking together in adversity, the New York spirit, that sort of stuff. But despite initial fears, this *wasn't* 9/11, as Tricia Romano commented in the *Village Voice*.

'Something strange happened to New York City last week. Yes, the power went out for 29 hours, but something else happened. The City's nightlife, though bereft of electricity, became fun. Like any night in the City, Thursday was to be the day of a billion events: DJs were supposed to spin, bands were to play. None of that happened. Instead, everyone had a giant block party. Tompkins Square Park turned into a blazing palace of drums and bonfires. People danced (without a cabaret licence) and drank alcohol and smoked "special cigarettes" out in the open...

'Most of us found the notion that New Yorkers were "sticking together" or supporting each other through the crisis silly. No, we were all too busy getting wasted in public to be bothered with fighting or squabbling.'

Among several 'blackout experiences' reported by Romano, one involved Ed Simmons and Tom Rowlands, the Chemical Brothers, who were in New York on a record-promotion visit. At the time of the power cut they were on the 14th floor of a midtown building, at a radio station, K-Rock. They'd just finished an interview and were about to get in the elevator when a record-company aide introduced them to some more station employees. While they chatted, the blackout happened; if they'd not been delayed they would have spent hours, maybe days, in the lift. Walking the 14 flights down the stairs, the two made their way to the stylish Mercer Hotel in SoHo, where they spent the night drinking in the lobby with a crowd of music-biz celebrities including Elvis Costello and Duran Duran's Nick Rhodes.

And the second of three nights at the Hammerstein Ballroom featuring Bob Dylan had to be postponed till later in the month. Life goes on.

AFTERWORD: THE BIG PARADE

The festive street-party spirit that the blackout inspired all over the City was in many ways a spontaneous manifestation of a New York trait that's deeply ingrained: a tradition of open-air events and parades. Even buskers and other street performers seem accepted as part of the human landscape rather than grudgingly tolerated as they are in many cities.

The most over-the-top parade of all, and certainly the most anticipated in New York and across the United States, is the annual Thanksgiving Day Parade organised for over 75 years by Macy's department store. Like many things in American life, it actually stems from European tradition.

In the 1920s many of Macy's department store employees were first-generation immigrants. Proud of their new American heritage, they wanted to celebrate the American holiday with the type of festival they loved in Europe. The employees marched along Broadway from Times Square down to 34th Street dressed as clowns, cowboys, knights and sheikhs. There were floats, professional bands and 25 live animals borrowed from the Central Park Zoo. And with an audience of over a quarter of a million people, the parade was an instant hit.

The familiar giant-size balloons first appeared in 1927 with the animated cartoon character Felix the Cat. In those days they would release the balloons and the lucky finder could claim a prize. And during the Depression the popularity of this diversion attracted bigger and bigger crowds: by 1934 over a million people were lining the route.

The event – which ceased for obvious reasons during World War II – was even covered by radio, though a running commentary would hardly have seemed remotely comparable! Then with the advent of television, it really took off as a national institution.

Now the parade, featuring incredible floats and bigger-than-ever character balloons – including, of course, Santa Claus – makes its way every year from the west side of Central Park at 77th Street down to Macy's store on 34th. It's undeniably kitsch, sentimental even, and overtly commercialised, but if you're around at Thanksgiving at the end of November, it's one of those all-American events that have a certain fascination for the overseas visitor – once at least.

The most famous Manhattan street parade as perceived on the other side of the Atlantic is, predictably, the St Patrick's Day bash. The 2003 parade was the 242nd, and with over 150,000 participants, claims to be the world's largest. Although it's celebrating a religious day, you'd hardly notice, as it marches up Fifth Avenue.

It's long been an occasion for the New York Irish population – and many more besides – to party, and there probably isn't a bigger day when green face paint, green food colouring, green nail polish and green clothes are on display. It's a day of historical pageantry too, with arcane bodies like the Ancient Order of Hibernians and scores of other Irish lodges and societies flying their flags. And, naturally, it's a time for music, from bagpipe bands and ceilidh groups to lone fiddlers.

The first official parade in the City was held in 1766 by Irishmen in a military unit recruited to serve in the American colonies. For the first few years of its existence, the parade was organised by military groups until after the war of 1812. At that point in time, Irish fraternal and beneficial societies took over the duties of hosting and sponsoring the event. But even now a unit of soldiers marches at the head of the parade, with the Irish 165th Infantry becoming the parade's primary escort.

The best places to see 'St Pat's' are reckoned to be on the north end of the route – it goes up Fifth Avenue from 44th to 86th Street – away from the midtown shopping area, a prime location if you get there early being the steps of the Metropolitan Museum of Art.

With the ethnic mix of New York, it's hardly surprising that parades and festivals on the lines of St Patrick's – though most not half as big – are a regular feature of life in the City, from Chinese New Year in late January to the Feast of San Gennaro held in Little Italy in mid-September.

San Gennaro, which is in the main a static street festival rather than grand parade, is the oldest celebration in that part of town. It was first held in 1926, and runs along Mulberry Street between Canal and Houston in what is now the remaining area of Little Italy. Although the religious aspect is celebrated with priest-led processions through the streets, the main feature is food. Fairground-type stalls line the street with game booths and rides, but these are eclipsed by the amazing array of Italian-based foodstuffs that are on sale, ready to eat.

Another big annual spectacle, even more dominated by its musical content than St Patrick's, is the Puerto Rican Day Parade, which follows the same path as the Irish event. And it's almost as big, with 100,000 participants marching or riding on exotic floats, dancing to the sounds of salsa, merengue, bomba, plena and Latin hip-hop. Added to that, hundreds of thousands more line the street waving flags, blowing whistles and salsa-dancing throughout the daylong event held in early June. Local politicians from the governor and mayor downwards always make a point of taking part: it's good inter-community public relations, and the Latino population represents a lot of votes! But if you're into Latin music of any kind, it's like one enormous mobile free festival.

Open-air music events *per se* are hugely popular, sometimes part of wider-ranging 'festivals' consisting mainly of club and concert gigs. The always-active scene based around the Sidewalk Café holds an annual Antifolk Fest every summer, featuring a huge outdoor 'Antihoot' with over two dozen New York performers, which takes place around Tompkins Square Park, the traditional centre for such local gatherings in the East Village.

The many parks across the City are a favourite setting for *al fresco* music. Washington Square Park in the West Village saw history in the making when, in the late 1950s and early '60s, it was the site of free-for-all music sessions that set alight a previously rather serious folk scene. In the '03 blackout it regained some of that former glory when spontaneous concerts continued through the starlit night.

Right in the middle of midtown, Bryant Park, behind the New York Public Library on Fifth Avenue, stages a summer season of classical, jazz and dance music, plus a Monday run of movies. With the evening sun glinting off the surrounding skyscrapers, the setting is unique.

Central Park has long been the location for concerts of every type of music, including of late the SummerStage free shows through June, July and August. And not to be outdone by Manhattan, the same period sees the Brooklyn Performing Arts Festival with outdoor events in Prospect Park.

AFTERWORD: BUSKIN' IT

The parks are great places for free entertainment of all kinds. On a rain-free day, every turn on the gently winding pathways of Central Park seems to reveal a musician or other 'performer' doing their thing, often not even busking for money, just happy to have a practice space and a ready-made audience. Having said that, New York's standard of regular buskers, the folks who do it for a living – professionals in other words – is particularly high. Anyone who's marvelled at the break-dancing crews that take over part of the concourse on the big subway-line intersections – Times Square, Grand Central, Union Square – will vouch for that.

It seems it's always been so. Talking to me about the 1950s phenomenon of doo-wop groups, and how they were reputed to sing on street corners and (for the better acoustics) in the stairwells of the housing project high-rises where they lived, singer and songwriter Paul Evans recalled seeing such outfits as he took the subway from Queens to midtown when he started hustling his songs in the Brill Building:

'I saw them on the subway…it's not a myth…and it wasn't just a black phenomenon, it was white and black, and the nice thing was even in those days in New York you saw mixed groups.'

There are still some marvellous doo-woppers to be heard operating on subway stations, even subway trains, and in shop doorways (the acoustics again) up and down Manhattan. Some are well into middle age now, clearly doing it from when it was the sharp teen thing, the rap of its day. Others are young kids who've learnt the craft from records, and maybe from fathers and grandfathers. Rock 'n' roll music handed down, father to son. Who'd have thought it?

Blues is intertwined with street musicians in its very history; many of its earliest practitioners were just that. Now-legendary bluesmen like Blind Boy Fuller and Junior Wells were playing the sidewalks before often meagrely paid recording dates preserved their names and music for posterity.

I'm not implying that another Robert Johnson lurks on the streets of New York, but the nature of the music lends itself to the solo musician armed only with an electric guitar and small portable amplifier. And there are some hot players around. I came across a guy recently on Mercer Street in SoHo. He was playing some pretty animated guitar, sounded like Hendrix. Scary thing was, as I came closer I could see he *looked* just like Hendrix. Dead ringer or clone, call it what you like.

But the most celebrated street player ever to walk the sidewalks of Manhattan was a musician who wasn't a busker, he didn't ask for donations, who went by the name of Moondog. Through much of the

1950s and '60s a permanent fixture along Sixth Avenue between 52nd and 56th Streets – they even called the corner of Sixth and 54th Moondog Corner – he entertained passers-by with poetry accompanied by his own home-made instruments.

Moondog – his real name was Louis Thomas Hardin – was an imposing figure, with a long beard and flowing robe, wearing a huge Viking helmet and carrying a tall spear. But few of the people who saw the blind musician on their way to and from the office every day would have suspected he was an accomplished recording artist, with albums of symphonic music, spoken poetry, and even some tracks recorded right there on the streets of Manhattan.

Born in Marysville, Kansas, in 1916, the self-taught street player released several albums on the Prestige label in the 1950s. During the beat era these records achieved cult status, no more so than *On The Streets Of New York*, an EP recorded *in situ* by producer and archivist Tony Schwartz. The original sleeve notes from the UK release on the London label give some idea of the atmosphere therein:

'The music heard in the EP is the result of recording and editing several hours of taped music in order to cull the most unusual. In this record, Moondog plays several new instruments – the "oo", the "utsu", and the "samisen". In one composition, recorded near the Hudson River piers, the tugboat and ocean liners' whistles and foghorns complement the composition, while Moondog plays and improvises; in another work, the actual sound of New York traffic – automobile motors, taxi horns, sounds of brakes, etc – is used similarly.'

Moondog could play, in addition to these bizarre instruments, piano, organ, clarinet, all the string instruments and most of the other woodwind instruments. His wife Suzuko was capable of singing in three octaves, and figured prominently in some of his recordings.

He came under an unexpected blaze of publicity when he took the pioneer rock 'n' roll DJ Alan Freed to court, forcing the latter to drop the name 'Moondog' from his radio show *Moondog's Rock 'n' Roll Party*.

In 1969 he was approached on the street by Columbia Records and recorded an orchestral album *Moondog*, which hovered, uniquely, between jazz and classical music.

Moondog moved to Germany in the mid '70s, where he continued to compose highly experimental works including the 1995 *Big Band* album and *Sax Pax For A Sax* in '97. His influence on avant-garde music was considerable, and the impact of his lifestyle on the New York beat and underground scenes significant. And he even had Janis Joplin cover one of his Prestige tracks, 'All Is Loneliness', with Big Brother & The Holding Company in the 1960s. He died in 2001.

I stopped to talk to Moondog on more than one occasion when he was there on the midtown streets, like hundreds of others did every day. I got the feeling that as far as he was concerned, notwithstanding the record collectors and avant-garde aficionados, these ordinary folk going about their daily business were his real public.

Moondog was blind, but he could see. That's been said of many a street musician since the beginning of time, albeit more often than not in a more literal sense. I had an encounter with a busker not so long ago, on the corner of Lafayette Street and Astor Place. He looked the archetypal be-bop player: black beret and shades, and playing a mean tenor sax. I took a couple of photos unobtrusively – he didn't seem to notice as the camera clicked and flashed – but before I could dig into my pocket for a dollar bill he'd taken the horn out of his mouth, rasped, 'You gonna help me out, buddy?', and swung back into 'Nights In Tunisia'.

If, like Moondog, his music had been recorded there and then it would have been against a backing track of car horns and police sirens, the rhythm section the incessant rattle of a nearby road drill, the antithesis of the antiseptic and sometimes sterile atmosphere of the recording studio.

I'm reminded here of the album *Charles Mingus Presents Charles Mingus*, at the beginning of which the great bass player requests his 'live' audience not to interrupt the music with the noise of applause, drinks or cash registers. It transpired the whole session took place in the sound-proofed silence of a studio, but Mingus wanted to recreate the atmosphere – including the dimmed lights – of a live date, albeit without the clutter of 'background' sound effects.

I was privileged to meet Mingus many years ago, introduced by the poet Ted Joans at a press reception held in Ungano's, a club long gone that used to be up on West 70th Street. A life-and-soul-of-the-party record-company employee interrupted us loudly as we chatted at the bar, back-slapping Mingus with a 'Hi, Charlie'.

Mingus, who didn't suffer fools gladly, replied curtly without looking at him, 'The name's Charles. You call a horse Charlie!'

AFTERWORD: WAKING AND WALKING

Waking up in New York, as I've mentioned earlier, is a matter of hitting the streets. Don't worry about hanging round that hotel room, whether it exudes the faded grandeur of the Algonquin or Gramercy, or the more down-to-earth quirky charms of a backpackers' bed-for-the-night like the Gershwin. In fact in the Gershwin, located just off Fifth Avenue on East 27th Street, there's not a lot in the bedroom to hang around for – basic amenities, 'popular with young student types who have little need for luxuries' as one guidebook puts it. You get the picture. What does distinguish the Gershwin from other budget accommodation in Manhattan, however, is the arty decor, with works by Lichtenstein and Warhol in the lobby, and poetry readings and stand-up comedy every evening. But who's going to stick around a hotel when you're in New York City? Like I said, a typical day visiting the Big Apple starts with hitting that street.

Despite my assurance in the Introduction that this wasn't going to be a book featuring do-it-yourself walking tours, I've outlined two walks that take in some places not touched on in the general sweep of my music-led text, but without mention of which any account of New York would be incomplete. But don't feel obliged to do the foot-slog; get to any place you fancy in any way you fancy, that's always been my motto.

Opinions vary, but my choice of area to stay is midtown-ish, anywhere between the Gramercy/Union Square area and south of Central Park. That way you're poised for the Village East and West, SoHo and the rest of downtown, while being in easy reach of the shops and museums, the Park, and anything further north that takes your fancy. And, as well as Broadway that cuts a diagonal swathe west to east through Columbus Circle down to where it crosses Fifth Avenue, you've got that other great thoroughfare, Fifth itself.

Broadway, it has to be remembered, stretches the whole 18km (11 mile) length of Manhattan Island, top to bottom, actually starting way north of that on the mainland of New York State. But it's in the midtown Theater District that it got its nickname of the Great White Way, when it became the glittering hub of New York showbusiness – and more specifically the Broadway musical – in the 1920s and '30s. The name has even been adopted for defining various kinds of theatre; plays can be described as Broadway, off Broadway or even off-off Broadway, depending on how far out of the commercial mainstream they might be considered.

My favourite midtown walk, however, given plenty of time, is the 36-block stretch of Fifth Avenue from the Flatiron Building at 23rd Street up to the Park at 59th. Not for restaurants, or music, or bars, but purely for walking and looking, browsing in a few shops maybe, soaking up the atmosphere of midtown and something of the visual essence of Manhattan.

The 20-storey Flatiron, so-called on account of its wedge shape, built on the fork where Broadway crosses Fifth, is one of the architectural wonders of New York; not least because it was the City's first skyscraper, and in 1903 one of the earliest buildings to use the interior steel-cage support that made high-rise possible.

The Flatiron stands facing Madison Square, a small park that was the site of the original Madison Square Garden, where prize fights, circuses and other lavish entertainments were staged before the 'Garden moved to its present location on Seventh Avenue in the 1960s. The new stadium meant the demolition of the historic Pennsylvania Station, an act that gave rise to the Landmarks Preservation Commission to prevent such urban vandalism in the future. The railroad terminal, which was rivalled only by Grand Central as an architectural masterpiece, was succeeded by the totally anonymous (in fact, from the street invisible) Penn Station, which is located directly beneath the 'Garden.

Walking up Fifth, the intersection with West 33rd Street (remembering that Fifth Avenue marks the demarcation between streets being East or West) brings us to the Art Deco splendour of the Empire State Building. More angular in style than the flamboyant Chrysler Building on nearby Lexington Avenue, it's one of the true icons of New York, its upper storeys floodlit at night with the colours varying according to the holiday or special occasion. And although there are always queues waiting in the lobby to take the elevator to the rooftop observation deck, the view from the top is an essential part of a first-time visit to the Big Apple.

Passing the magnificent steps up to the New York Public Library, also on the west side of Fifth, glancing east down 42nd Street you'll see the Chrysler in more complete perspective a couple of blocks away than the neck-craning view from Lexington, though the latter is more overpoweringly dramatic.

Further up the avenue we come to the Rockefeller Center, the Art Deco complex of hard-edged rectangular buildings dominated by the sleekly narrow-looking General Electric Building, formerly the RCA Building. The building looks 'narrow' because it's far deeper than it is wide, and gazing through the avenue of smaller buildings leading to the open-air Plaza it seems even more so. The central Plaza is one of the most successful open spaces in New York, with the space in front sunken below street level providing a skating rink and, when the occasion demands it, a live-performance space. And by way of contrast, right across the avenue from the center stands the 19th century neo-Gothic extravagance of St Patrick's Cathedral.

This part of Fifth Avenue is very much about shops and shopping. Saks, Bergdorf Goodman, H&M, the lavishly decorative Henri Bendel add up to a shopaholic's paradise – and that's just the department stores. And as far as the time-honoured occupation of shoppin' for clothes is concerned, you need go no further – well, as long as you've got the finance for some serious designer labels. Fendi, Gucci, Louis Vuitton, Versace, they're all on Fifth, with Burberry, Chanel, Dior just on the side streets, not to mention jewellery emporiums that include Cartier, Bulgari and the overtly celebrated Tiffany.

Post-modernism in architecture was partly a reaction to the starkness of the glass-and-concrete modernism of the 1960s and '70s, an attempt to regain some of the decorative warmth inherent in the Art Deco flourishes of buildings like the Chrysler (though considered ultra-modern in their time). A typical example is the Trump Tower, the world's tallest residential building, resplendent in all its gold-topped vulgarity at Fifth and 56th Street. Also visible is the splendid flippancy of the Sony (formerly AT&T) Building on Madison Avenue, with its rooftop façade looking like something that's fallen off a Chippendale chest of drawers.

At 59th Street we hit the Park, the most popular and populated part, where the horse-drawn buggies line up around Grand Army Plaza at the southeast corner, and winter ice-skaters crowd on to the Wollman Rink.

Proceeding up Fifth Avenue there's a walk for another day, along the east side of the Park, where shopaholism gives way to culture vulturism. You're at the start of 'Museum Mile', which includes the Frick Collection, the Whitney Museum of American Art just a block over on Madison, the Metropolitan Museum of Art, whose huge collection covers over 140,000 sq m (1.5 million sq ft), the Guggenheim – Frank Lloyd Wright's amazing spiral gallery which still looks ultra-modern after more than 40-odd years – the Cooper-Hewitt, the Jewish Museum, the Museum of the City of New York and finally Spanish Harlem's Museo del Barrio.

The nerve centre of much of what New York is all about of course, is to be found in the civic and financial district downtown. A great way to catch the flavour of this historic area is a walk starting at Battery Park just along the Promenade from the Staten Island Ferry Terminal, up through the lower part of Broadway and Wall Street to the City Hall, Municipal Building and US and County Courthouses, all near the entrance to the Brooklyn Bridge.

The Battery Park Promenade is now the open stage for street performers and buskers, while the Park itself plays host to touring events and free outdoor music on summer evenings, getting its name from the battery of cannons that protected the Manhattan shoreline from possible attack from the British in the years following the War of Independence. Castle Clinton, to be found inside the Park, was built in 1811 for the same reason.

Walking up through the middle of the Park we get to Bowling Green, the City's oldest surviving park, with the magnificent Beaux Arts-style US Custom House, which houses the National Museum of the American Indian. The northern point of this grassy triangle touches the very bottom end of Broadway, along which, two blocks north, is Trinity Church. A 19th-century Gothic Revival building, with its 80m (264ft) brownstone tower, it was, until the 1890s, Manhattan's tallest.

A block further up Broadway we can see the Equitable Building, which, with its sheer 40-storey sides and no inclined setbacks to let in light and air to surrounding streets, led in 1916 to legislation governing the shape of skyscrapers from then on.

Opposite Trinity Church is Wall Street, nerve centre of US commerce and site of the New York Stock Exchange, on the right walking from Broadway. Further on down, over Nassau Street, is the Federal Hall National Memorial. On the outside is a replica of the Parthenon; the original hall was where George Washington was inaugurated as the country's first president in 1789, the present building dating from 1842.

Walking up Nassau and taking a left along Fulton brings you back to Broadway and St Paul's Chapel, built in 1766 New York's only surviving building from pre-Revolutionary days. Amazingly, both St Paul's and Trinity also survived the Word Trade Center disaster, only a block to the west over Church Street.

A little further up Broadway stands one of the most magnificent buildings in all of New York, the Woolworth Building dating from 1913, when it was (briefly) the tallest in the world. A skyscraper version of a Gothic cathedral, it rises nearly 250m (800ft) and has been called the Mozart of skyscrapers. Just check out the lobby.

Opposite the Woolworth is City Hall Park, with its elegant namesake building in the northern end. It's hard to imagine now that when it was built in 1812, it stood at the City's northernmost edge. Facing it along Park Row, which runs along the east side of the Park, stands the Municipal Building, the bureaucratic functions within merely an extension of City Hall, which it resembles design-wise.

By now we're almost in the lower part of Chinatown, and, to the east, within walking distance of Brooklyn Bridge. Taking a left off Park Row up Centre Street towards Foley Square, we pass two more neo-Classic buildings, familiar from many a crime movie or television series: the United States Courthouse and the New York County Courthouse, the latter used most famously in Sidney Lumet's *Twelve Angry Men*.

Mention of 9/11 takes me back to those dark events and their aftermath. I was in New York in October '01 while the City was still in a state of shock, numbed by what had happened less than two months earlier. I had a meeting downtown, near Church Street, which bordered the gaping hole in the landscape that had been dubbed Ground Zero. The most shocking aspect for me at the time was the smoke, which was still rising from the crater out of which the ruins were being excavated, and the acrid smell of smouldering material that came with it. And the sirens of ambulances, six weeks after the holocaust, ferrying to and fro from the site where hundreds of bodies remained buried.

My thoughts move to 'Where were you when…?' When the Twin Towers fell, I was being evacuated from the high-rise office complex in London's Canary Wharf. We'd seen the planes hit on the internet; next thing the whole area was told to go home.

Another tragic New York event that elicits the same question was when John Lennon was shot dead outside his home in the Dakota Building. In England we heard it on early-morning radio as we got up, unbelieving, hoping we were still asleep, a bad dream. The next time I was in New York, which was nearly 12 years after the Lennon assassination in 1980, the area of Central Park that edges onto the east side of the Dakota on the smart Upper West Side, had become a shrine – official.

The centrepiece is the 'Imagine' mosaic in the small space now labelled Strawberry Fields. This title for the area seemed odd to me, given that the real place on which the song was based is also a well-known site of Beatle-inspired pilgrimage in Liverpool. The round plaque-like mosaic is always festooned with small floral tributes, candles, poems and paintings, that get removed and dumped daily by the Park Department.

I was with my family, and we walked by the side entrance of the Dakota on West 72nd Street, glancing rather than peering into the gloomy entrance gate where Lennon was murdered, past the ever-present security guard. It was hot. We'd been watching the Sunday morning amateur baseball just earlier, a guy selling us cold beers from a freezer bag in clear contravention of the Park's no-alcohol rule.

We looked up at the imposing Gothic presence of the Dakota one more time. Life goes on. My son Jake bought a round of hot dogs from a stand and we went on our way, above us only sky.

Appendix 1

Sounds, Tastes And Things To Do

TWENTY OF NEW YORK'S HOTTEST MUSIC VENUES

APOLLO THEATER
The most celebrated Harlem venue for blues, R&B and soul.
253 West 125th Street
Tel: 212-749-5838

ARLENE GROCERY (See Map 1)
Features everything from Irish rock to folk.
95 Stanton Street between Ludlow and Orchard Streets
Tel: 212-358-1633

ARTHUR'S TAVERN (See Map 1)
Jazz and blues venue of 60 years' standing.
57 Grove Street between Bleecker Street and Seventh Avenue South
Tel: 212-675-6879

BIRDLAND
Jazz venue featuring some of the biggest names around.
315 West 44th Street between Eighth and Ninth Avenues
Tel: 212-581-3080

BITTER END (See Map 1)
Legendary club since the early days of the Village folk scene.
147 Bleecker Street at Thompson
Tel: 212-673-7030

BOTTOM LINE (See Map 1)
Rock and jazz cabaret-style venue for over 25 years.
15 West 4th Street at Mercer Street
Tel: 212-228-6300

BOWERY BALLROOM (See Map 1)
Elegant venue with balcony and downstairs lounge.
6 Delancey Street between the Bowery and Chrystie Street
Tel: 212-533-2111

CBGB (See Map 1)
Legendary home of punk rock.
315 Bowery at Bleecker Street
Tel: 212-982-4052

THE KNITTING FACTORY (See Map 1)
Avant-garde, jazz and indie bands.
74 Leonard Street between Broadway and Church Street
Tel: 212-219-3055

LUNA LOUNGE (See Map 1)
All the best new bands.
171 Ludlow Street between Houston and Stanton Streets
Tel: 212-260-2323

LUXX (See Map 2)
Fantasy environment featuring local, national and international acts.
256 Grand Street, Williamsburg, Brooklyn
Tel: 718-599-1000

MAXWELL'S
Hoboken club concentrating on new names with some established acts.
1039 Washington Street, Hoboken, New Jersey
Tel: 201-798-0406

MERCURY LOUNGE (See Map 1)
Cutting-edge names in venue famous for its near-perfect acoustics.
217 East Houston Street at Avenue A
Tel: 212-260-4700

NORTHSIX (See Map 2)
DJs, live bands, movies, dance and performance art.
66 North 6th Street, Williamsburg, Brooklyn
Tel: 718-599-5103

PETE'S CANDY STORE (See Map 2)
Voted Brooklyn's best bar with live music seven nights a week.
709 Lorimer Street, Williamsburg, Brooklyn
Tel: 718-302-3770

SIDEWALK CAFÉ (See Map 1)
Hub of the antifolk scene.
94 Avenue A at 6th Street
Tel: 212-473-7373

SOB's (See Map 1)
Major club venue for Latin and world music.
204 Varick Street at West Houston Street
Tel: 212-243-4940

VILLAGE UNDERGROUND (See Map 1)
Eclectic mix of major-name rock, soul and country-rock acts.
130 West 3rd Street between MacDougal Street and Sixth Avenue
Tel: 212-777-7745

VILLAGE VANGUARD (See Map 1)
Legendary jazz venue.
178 Seventh Avenue South at Perry Street
Tel: 212-255-4037

WARSAW (See Map 2)
Cutting-edge new names plus established stars.
Polish National Home, 261 Driggs Avenue, Brooklyn
Tel: 718-387-5252

TWENTY BARS, DELIS, DINERS AND RESTAURANTS FOR THE TASTE OF NEW YORK

CEDAR TAVERN
Historic '50s watering hole for the beat generation when it was at Number 24, it still has lots of atmosphere and is dark whatever time of day. Serves decent bar-style food.
82 University Place between 11th and 12th Streets
Tel: 212-929-9089

CHUMLEY'S
Another literary legacy, with a range of seriously strong beers and a pub-food menu.
86 Bedford Street between Barrow and Commerce Streets
Tel: 212-675-4449

THE COFFEE SHOP
Lively bar and Brazilian-based restaurant.
29 Union Square West at 16th Street
Tel: 212-243-7969

DEAN & DeLUCA
Fabulous foodstore that sells simply the best of almost anything you'd
want to eat and great just to look at.
560 Broadway at Prince Street
Tel: 212-431-1691

EMPIRE DINER
Classic Deco-style diner with a menu that extends from the usual diner
fare; open 24 hours.
210 Tenth Avenue at West 22nd Street
Tel: 212-243-2736

FANELLI'S CAFÉ
Friendly – and usually busy – SoHo dive bar, it also serves basic dishes.
94 Prince Street at Mercer Street
Tel: 212-226-9412

GRAND CENTRAL OYSTER BAR
A legend of old New York, lunchtimes are usually packed with locals
sampling the diverse choice of fish and seafood.
Grand Central Terminal, Lower Concourse, 42nd Street at Park Avenue
Tel: 212-490-6650

JOHN'S PIZZERIA
One of the most famous pizza places in the City, and rightly so.
278 Bleecker Street at Jones Street
Tel: 212-243-1680

JULES' BISTRO
Good French cooking, with live jazz and a local clientele, including French
expats, always a good sign.
65 St Mark's Place between First and Second Avenues
Tel: 212-477-5560

KATZ'S DELICATESSEN
Famous for the memorable scene in *When Harry Met Sally* and, equally, its superb kosher nosh.
205 East Houston at Ludlow Street
Tel: 212-254-2246

McSORLEY'S OLD ALE HOUSE
You're here for the beer – it's the only booze they serve – and the inexpensive lunch snacks.
15 East 7th Street between Second and Third Avenues
Tel: 212-473-9148

MONTE'S
For superb home-made pasta and seafood specialities, one of the premier Italian restaurants in Greenwich Village.
97 MacDougal Street between Bleecker and 3rd Streets
Tel: 212-228-9194

NATHAN'S FAMOUS
At the Coney Island beach and fairground site, Nathan's is famous for its hot dogs – and for the annual Nathan's Famous Fourth Of July Hot Dog Eating Contest.
1310 Surf Avenue at Stillwell Avenue, Coney Island, Brooklyn
Tel: 718-946-2202

ODEON
Cutting-edge trendy when it opened in 1980 and still popular, with a solid reputation for good, imaginative cooking.
145 West Broadway between Duane and Thomas Streets
Tel: 212-233-0507

PETE'S TAVERN
One of the oldest bars in NY, with good beer and better-than-average menu.
129 East 18th Street at Irving Place
Tel: 212-473-7676

THE RED FLAME
If you're staying in midtown, the place to go for the classic, short-order American breakfast. Justifiably popular with locals and visitors alike.
67 West 44th Street between Fifth and Sixth Avenues
Tel: 212-869-3965

RUDY'S BAR & GRILL
One of the last of its kind, a no-frills dive bar with lots of character and a great jukebox.
627 Ninth Avenue between 44th and 45th Streets
Tel: 212-974-9169

SYLVIA'S
Noted worldwide for its soul food, and certainly the most celebrated eatery in Harlem.
328 Lenox Avenue between 126th and 127th Streets
Tel: 212-996-0660

UNION SQUARE CAFÉ
Upmarket restaurant: fine food, beautifully prepared, reservations essential.
21 East 16th Street, between Fifth Avenue and Union Square
Tel: 212-243-4020

ZABAR'S
The ultimate New York deli and food market. A mind-boggling – and mouth-watering – food extravaganza, including sausages, breads, cheeses, coffees and its speciality, smoked fish.
2245 Broadway at 80th Street
Tel: 212-787-2000

TWENTY PLACES FOR THE NEW YORK EXPERIENCE

ANNEX FLEA MARKET
They say a lot of a city's character can be found in its junk. This regular market is always worth a visit, along with the indoor Garage market nearby. Sixth Avenue between 24th and 26th Streets, Saturday and Sunday
Tel: 212-243-5343

BARNES & NOBLE
The biggest bookstore in America, and the flagship of the huge B&N chain, this branch on the north side of Union Square is just one of 20 in NYC alone. If you're a bookaholic, pig out!
33 East 17th Street between Broadway and Park Avenue South
Tel: 212-253-0810

BASEBALL
You don't have to support the Mets at Shea or the New York Yankees at Yankee Stadium to get a buzz from this quintessential New York sport. Just sit in any bar when there's a big game on, it'll be there on the TV, or watch the amateur teams in Central Park on a Sunday.

Shea Stadium
123-01 Roosevelt Avenue at 126th Street, Flushing, Queens
Tel: 718-507-8499

Yankee Stadium
River Avenue at 161st Street, the Bronx
Tel: 718-293-6000

BROOKLYN BRIDGE
Just stroll across to Brooklyn Heights Promenade for a wonderful vista of Manhattan, or take the subway to High Street Brooklyn and walk back. Subway to City Hall-Brooklyn Bridge (Manhattan) or High Street (Brooklyn)

CENTRAL PARK
Strolling in Central Park can be magical all year round, watching the skaters in winter and the skateboarders in summer, with the skyline ever-present beyond the trees.
Bordered by Central Park West (Eighth Avenue), Central Park North (110th Street), Fifth Avenue and Central Park South (West 59th Street)

CHINATOWN
South of Broome Street between Broadway and the Bowery, and centred on Canal Street, it's almost another country, with the largest Chinese population outside Asia.

CHRYSLER BUILDING
For any fan of Art Deco, probably the most beautiful building in the world. Just stand and stare.
405 Lexington Avenue at 42nd Street

EMPIRE STATE BUILDING
It's a tourist trap, but you have got to go up top for unforgettable views of the City.
350 Fifth Avenue between 33rd and 34th Streets
Tel: 212-736-3100

FLATIRON BUILDING
Completed in 1903, one of New York's first real 'skyscrapers' using an interior steel-cage support, it gets its name from its shape, built as it is on the acute angle where Broadway crosses Fifth Avenue.
175 Fifth Avenue between 22nd and 23rd Streets

GRAND CENTRAL TERMINAL
The magnificent 90-year-old Main Concourse, a vast pedestrian area dominated by three 23m (75ft) high windows, is a must-see even if you're not taking the train.
From 42nd to 44th Streets between Vanderbilt and Lexington Avenues
Tel: 212-697-1245

GUGGENHEIM MUSEUM
Frank Lloyd Wright's amazing spiral gallery still looks ultra-modern after more than 40-odd years.
1071 Fifth Avenue at 89th Street
Tel: 212-423-3500

HELICOPTER FLIGHT
Forget the cost, definitely the ultimate way to see Manhattan. Treat yourself!
VIP Heliport, West 30th Street and Twelfth Avenue or Downtown Manhattan Heliport, at Pier 6 and the East River
Tel: 702-233-1627

METROPOLITAN MUSEUM OF ART
The huge collection featuring every conceivable genre and period of art covers over 140,000 sq m (1.5 million sq ft), so don't expect to do it in a day – or a week for that matter.
1000 Fifth Avenue at 82nd Street
Tel: 212-535-7710

MUSEUM OF MODERN ART (MoMA)
One of the finest collections of modern art in the world, and while it's temporarily (until 2005) in Queens during its 53rd Street refurbishment, the view of Manhattan from the overground subway line is worth the trip in itself.
33rd Street at Queens Boulevard, Long Island City, Queens
Tel: 212-708-9400

PARADES
New Yorkers love a parade, and whether it's Macy's Thanksgiving bash, St Patrick's Day, Puerto Rican Day or one of a score of others, they're always worth catching.

RADIO CITY MUSIC HALL
The entrance lobby is a classic of Art Deco design; ring if you want to
go on the guided tour.
West 50th Street at Sixth Avenue
Tel: 212-247-4777

ROCKEFELLER CENTER
The first complex in the world to integrate offices, shops and entertainment
facilities, the center is another classic example of the Art Deco architecture
for which New York is famous. In front of the dominant General Electric
(formerly RCA) building, passers-by on Fifth Avenue can watch the skaters
or take in some live music, in the huge sunken concourse.
From 48th to 51st Streets between Fifth and Sixth Avenues

ST PATRICK'S CATHEDRAL
Juxtaposed – and dwarfed – by skyscrapers, this Gothic Revival building
was once the most imposing building on this stretch of Fifth Avenue,
and is still the tallest cathedral in the United States.
Fifth Avenue between 50th and 51st Streets
Tel: 212-753-2261

STATEN ISLAND FERRY
The cheapest (ie free) ride in town, running 24 hours, with spectacular
views of downtown Manhattan and the Statue of Liberty.
South Ferry Terminal, South Street at Whitehall Street
Tel: 718-815-2628

TIFFANY & CO
OK, so you can't get breakfast here, and you probably can't afford
the jewellery, accessories and watches on show either, but it makes
for great browsing.
727 Fifth Avenue at 57th Street
Tel: 212-755-8000

Appendix 2

Hotels, Getting There And Getting Around

SOME NEW YORK HOTELS

THE ALGONQUIN
Still rather grand, this was one of New York's literary landmarks when writers gathered here in the '20s and '30s. The hotel's Blue Bar, with Sinatra prominent on the jukebox, is a hark back to another age.
59 West 44th Street between Fifth and Sixth Avenues
Tel: 212-840-6800

CHELSEA HOTEL
A legendary address, where guests and residents have ranged from Mark Twain and Dylan Thomas to – infamously – Sid Vicious and Nancy Spungen. There's now a smart-set cocktail lounge, Serena, in the basement.
222 West 23rd Street between Seventh and Eighth Avenues
Tel: 212-243-3700

HOTEL EDISON
In the heart of the Theater District and famous for its Art Deco lobby, the Edison has been renovated but the room rates remain reasonable.
228 West 47th Street at Broadway
Tel: 212-840-5000

THE GERSHWIN HOTEL
Popular with students and backpackers, a lively joint in a good location, with poetry readings and stand-up comedy – and shared dorms if you can't afford a private room.
7 East 27th Street between Fifth and Madison Avenues
Tel: 212-545-8000

GRAMERCY PARK HOTEL
The faded grandeur has recently seen a refurbishment, but the piano bar still maintains its louche charm. Guests get a key to the adjoining Gramercy Park.
2 Lexington Avenue at 21st Street
Tel: 212-475-4320

HOTEL 17
The ultimate in shabby chic, with 1950s wallpaper and a shared bathroom, it's been the location for a Madonna photo shoot and Woody Allen's *Manhattan Murder Mystery*.
225 East 17th Street between Second and Third Avenues
Tel: 212-475-2845

THE HUDSON
Trendy – and pricey – designer hotel with celebrity clientele to match.
356 West 58th Street between Eighth and Ninth Avenues
Tel: 212-554-6000

WASHINGTON SQUARE HOTEL
Inexpensive no-frills Greenwich Village hotel, with breakfast included in the rates.
103 Waverly Place between Fifth and Sixth Avenues
Tel: 212-777-9515

GETTING THERE

BY AIR
NYC is served by three major airports: JFK, Newark and La Guardia.

John F Kennedy International Airport
The main international airport serving NYC.
Tel: 718-244-4444

Newark Liberty International Airport
A little further from Manhattan than JFK, the New Jersey airport also connects internationally and is still within easy reach of the City.
Tel: 973-961-6000

La Guardia Airport
Oriented to business passengers on domestic and Canadian routes.
Tel: 718-476-5000

The trip from each airport into Manhattan is well served with rail and bus links. The subway ride from JFK can be tedious, however, often taking up to two hours, but extremely cheap at $2 (£1.25). Although further afield, the train and monorail link from Newark only takes about 40 minutes.

A yellow cab (don't be tempted by the ubiquitous unlicensed drivers touting for business) costs a flat $35 (£22) from JFK plus the tunnel toll (about $3.50/£2.20 – you may need to have cash ready) and tip ($4 or $5/£2.50 or £3). Coming back from Manhattan there's no flat fare, so it varies with the journey time.

Likewise, there's no flat fare to or from Newark; a cab will cost around $45 (£28) plus toll and tip.

BY RAIL
New York City has two major train stations in Manhattan, and is served by the long-distance Amtrak system, plus more local routes covered by Long Island Rail Road, Metro-North linking with towns north of Manhattan, New Jersey Transit and the fully automated low-cost Port Authority Trans Hudson (PATH) also for destinations in New Jersey.

Grand Central Terminal
The hub of Metro-North, running services to stations across New York State and Connecticut.
42nd to 44th Streets between Vanderbilt and Lexington Avenues. Subway to 42nd Street-Grand Central

Penn Station
For Long Island Rail Road, New Jersey Transit plus cross-country Amtrak trains.
31st to 33rd Streets between Seventh and Eighth Avenues. Subway to 34th Street-Penn Station

BY BUS
Cheaper, though usually a longer and less comfortable journey than by train, the major long-distance bus services are Greyhound and Peter Pan.

Greyhound Trailways
The most famous bus line in America, serving every part of the country.
Tel: 800-231-2222

Peter Pan
It covers the northeast, and tickets can also be used on Greyhound buses.
Tel: 800-343-9999

Both these services, and most out-of-town buses, come and go from:
Port Authority Bus Terminal
625 Eighth Avenue between 40th and 42nd Streets
Tel: 212-564-8484

GETTING AROUND

SUBWAY

The New York subway is easy to use and certainly the quickest way to travel in the City. Routes in Manhattan roughly reflect the morth–south street grid system, so are simple to follow on the map. Most stations are named after the street and avenue numbers where they are situated, but look out for separate entrances to uptown or downtown platforms at some locations.

Travelling is even easier with a Metrocard, which gives you a set number of rides depending on how much you pay for it (and can be 'topped up' when it expires); it also applies to the buses and can be used by more than one person. Or there's a one-day or seven-day pass, which gives you unlimited rides. And it's cheap; as with the bus, a $2 (£1.25) flat fare takes you anywhere in the City.

BUS

Bus routes are as easy to follow, and if you need to change from an uptown/downtown line to crosstown or vice versa, simply ask for a free transfer (lasting an hour) to continue your travel. You can also get a free transfer on to the subway if you're using a Metrocard. And don't forget, if you don't have a Metrocard, buses only accept coins – no notes.

TAXI

Taxis in New York are probably the most easily available in any city in the world. There are about 12,000 roaming the streets for fares and the light on the roof tells you if one's free. There's a maximum of four passengers allowed, three into the back and one up front. The main thing to remember is to jump in the cab before you tell the driver where you're heading; they don't like loitering. Always try where possible to give the cross-street address; for instance, '5th and 57th' rather than 'Tiffanys at 727 Fifth Avenue'. Even outside the numbered grid, 'Ludlow between Houston and Stanton' will suffice to get you to the Luna Lounge.

WALKING
New York, particularly Manhattan, is generally very walkable. In the 'grid' it's possible to calculate distances, keeping in mind that 20 avenue (north–south) or ten street (east–west) blocks are equal to 1 mile (1.6km). This doesn't apply, of course, to parts of Greenwich Village or lower Manhattan, or indeed to the outer boroughs.

DRIVING
If you're a visitor – and a lot of locals would agree, too – don't even think about it. The congestion's bad enough already, parking's a nightmare and public transport and/or taxis – unlike, say LA – are good enough to get you anywhere.

Bibliography

BANGS, Lester – *Blondie* (Omnibus Press, US/UK 1980)

BETROCK, Alan – *Girl Groups: The Story Of A Sound* (Delilah Communications, US 1982)

BOCKRIS, Victor – *Beat Punks* (Da Capo, US 2000)

BOCKRIS, Victor/MALANGA, Gerard – *Uptight: The Velvet Underground Story* (Omnibus Press, UK 1983)

COLBY, Paul – *The Bitter End: Hanging Out At America's Nightclub* (Cooper Square, US 2002)

COLEGRAVE, Stephen/SULLIVAN, Chris – *Punk: A Life Apart* (Cassell, UK 2001)

EVANS, Mike – *NYC Rock* (Sanctuary, UK 2003)

GEORGE-WARREN, Holly (contributor) – *New York City: Traditions* (Hamlyn, UK 1998)

GUERIN, Louise (contributor) – *New York City: Traditions* (Hamlyn, UK 1998)

HAJDU, David – *Positively Fourth Street* (Farrar, Straus and Giroux, US 2001)

HELMSTROM, John – *Punk: The Original* (Trans-High Publishing, US 1996)

KING, Francis – *The Warhol Look* (Bullfinch/AWM, US 1998)

MORGAN, Bill – *The Beat Generation In New York: A Walking Tour Of Jack Kerouac's City* (City Lights, US 1997)

SHAPIRO, Nat/HENTOFF, Nat – *Hear Me Talkin' To You* (Dover Books, US 1966)

SHELDON, Robert – *No Direction Home* (Da Capo, US 1986)

SLOMAN, Larry 'Ratso' – *On The Road With Bob Dylan* (Helter Skelter, UK 2002)

SOUNES, Howard – *Down The Highway* (Doubleday, UK 2001)

VALENTINE, Gary – *New York Rocker: My Life In The Blank Generation* (Sidgwick & Jackson, UK 2002)

VICKERS, Graham (contributor) – *New York City: Traditions* (Hamlyn, UK 1998)

WALLOCK, Leonard (editor) – *New York: Culture Capital Of The World 1940–1965* (Rizzoli, US 1988)

Plus the following publications and websites:
antifolk.net, *Billboard*, cbgb.com, *Circuit*, cmj.com, hotelchelsea.com, knittingfactory.com, *LCD* magazine, lunalounge.com, matadorrecords.com, mergerecords.com, mtve.com, *New Musical Express, New York Herald Tribune, New York Magazine*, newyorkmetro.com, *New York Observer, New York Times, Punk* magazine, *Rolling Stone*, rudysbarandgrill.com, subpop.com, *Sunday Times, Time Out New York, Village Voice*, wfmu.org.

Index

Chumley's 12, 46,
50–1, 174
Churchill, Winston S
93
city blues 123
City Club 87
City Hall 168, 169
City Hall Park 169
Clancy Brothers, The
47
Clarke, Arthur C 37
Clash, The 74, 106,
107, 108, 127
Clinton, Bill 112
Clinton, Chelsea 112
Clinton, Hillary 112
clubs 21, 62, 144
20 hottest music
venues 171–4
(see also by name)
Cockburn, Bruce 55
Coffee Shop, The
(Union Square) 12,
174
Cogs, The 142
Cohen, Leonard 37
Colby, Paul 12, 57–67
Coleman, Cy 60
Coleman, Steve 72
Collins, Judy 63
Collins, Phil 17–18
Cologne Cathedral 24
colour bar 59–60
Coltrane, John 48
Columbia Records
117, 163
Columbus Circle 165
comic books 106
community boards 80
Con Fullum Band, The
124
Coney Island High 81

Connolly, Billy 95
Cooper-Hewitt Design
Museum 14, 168
Corea, Chick 62
Corner Bistro 89
Corso, Gregory 10,
37, 51
Coryell, Larry 62
Costello, Elvis 74,
116, 158
Country, BlueGrass and
Blues (see CBGB)
country blues 123
country music 123
County Courthouse
168, 169
crack 117
Crenshaw, Marshall 55
Crow, Sheryl 26, 52

Dakota Building 170
Damned, The 106
Dan Dare 106
Dashboard
Percussional 153
Davies, Dave 153
Davis, Miles 48, 60,
66–7, 71
Dawson, Kimya 150
Dead Boys, The 127
Dean & De Luca 90,
175
DeCrow, Karen 100
Dee Dee 38
Defector III 74
Delancy Street 132
delis 90–1, 174–7
department stores 167
Depeche Mode 138
designer labels 167
Detroit 9
Devo 127

Dick James Publishing
137
Dillon, Matt 110
Dine, Jim 37
diners 86–8, 174–7
Dirt, Johnny 12,
29–30
DMZ 153
The Dolls 83
Dom Theatre 98
Don Hill's 83
doo-wop groups 162
Dorf, Michael 69–73,
76
driving in New York
187
drugs and drug dealing
104, 109, 117
Dubway Recording
Studios 156
Duchamp, Marcel 93
Dutch West India Co
93
Dylan, Bob 8, 10, 26,
37, 110, 123, 148,
158
in Greenwich Village
47–8, 51, 64–7, 108
walking tour 46

Eagles, The 136
Earl, Jack 12, 29–33
East Village 34, 49,
50, 98–9, 104–5,
116, 117, 119, 121,
148–9, 156
East Village Other
(newspaper) 98–9
eating out 86–91
Edinburgh Festival
fringe 49
Edison Hotel 91, 182

MAP 1 - LOWER MANHATTAN

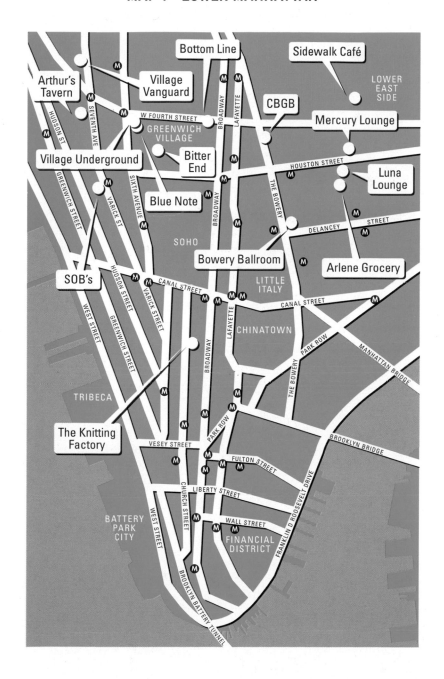

Maps

LOWER MANHATTAN AND BROOKLYN
The majority of New York's live music venues are located in lower Manhattan and Brooklyn. The following pages pinpoint the whereabouts of a selection of the hottest venues discussed in this book.

MAP 2 - BROOKLYN

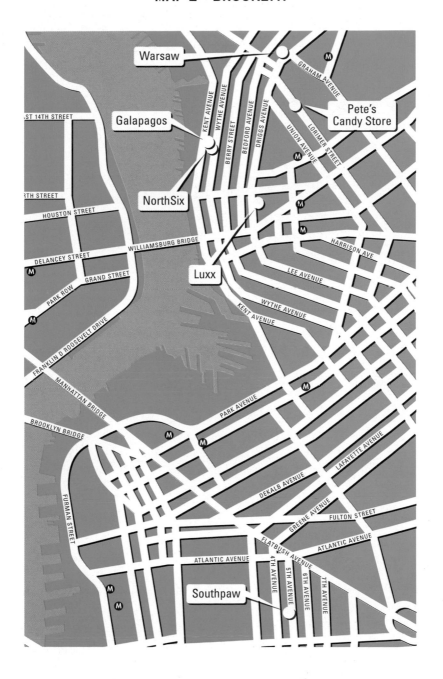